TAROT-CARD

SPREAD

READER

Doris Chase Doane
and King Keyes

PARKER PUBLISHING COMPANY, INC.
West Nyack, N.Y.

LIBRARY OF CONGRESS
CATALOG CARD NUMBER: 67-19976

Second Printing.....May, 1968

PRINTED IN THE UNITED STATES OF AMERICA
B & P

*B*ecause everything which exists has an
astrological correspondence which is
also associated with a tarot card, by
selecting the proper factors, any
physical or occult problem may be
solved by the use of the tarot. . . . What
the tarot can be made to reveal is limited
only by the capacity of understanding of
the person using it.

C. C. ZAIN

DEDICATION

To all those brave souls, who, amidst
enormous prejudice, have searched for,
are investigating, and will continue
to seek out the basic truths of nature's
laws, this book is sincerely dedicated.

WHAT THIS BOOK CAN DO FOR YOU

O ver the years, different types of Tarot Cards have been published as well as tarot books dealing with philosophy. The great lack in this field has been a how-to-do-it approach, telling the reader the manner in which to spread, and *interpret* the cards. Here you are given information which you can turn to on the spur of the moment! This unique book, the only one of its kind, demonstrates ways for you to use your Tarot cards.

Many different packs of tarot cards have come into existence, and this book describes the reasons for this. It also clearly describes the cards and their use as correlated to the *authentic, ancient meanings*—fragments of which began to appear during the past century after having gone underground before the Dark Ages. With the unique sections entitled "Key Phrases for the 78 Tarot Cards" and "Astrological Symbolism," the information can be readily applied to tarot cards of any design.

This is possible because symbols are the universal language. Any type of tarot cards can be used to lay the spreads demonstrated here. Once the meanings of symbols are mastered, the keywords listed for each card can be used to interpret any tarot pack, regardless of design. An insert containing a full set of Tarot cards is in this book, and you might wish to cut the cards out of these insert sheets. However, a full-sized professional deck of the Egyptian Tarot Cards, imprinted on sturdy stock, can be ordered from The Church of Light, Dept. PH, Box 1525, Los Angeles, California 90053, at $4.50 postpaid.

This book will round out any occult library. Through its use, the kabalist will be enabled to bring more precision and depth of understanding to his studies. The neophyte, or beginner, who meditates psychically will find unlimited spiritual topics for meditation. And the mystic and occultist will find surprising enlightenment as regards the whys and wherefores of his beliefs and practices.

It is not necessary to be a student of the occult arts to understand and use the self-help offered in this book. To keep abreast of an ever-widening interest in astrology, however, the layman will gain an insight into the subject and discover a fascinating hobby, which could prove to be his key to a wider popularity with friends and acquaintances, and a far more fulfilled life in every respect.

Astrophiles, students and professional astrologers will discover unlimited combinations in handy reference form which will stimulate and broaden their awareness, leading them to new vistas of astrological interpretation.

Your subconscious mind understands a lot more about symbolism than you realize. Symbolism is a universal language, one that is grasped by people all over the world, regardless of their native tongues. Although symbolism may seem to be a mystical subject, its universal stamp is seen upon every hand in our daily lives .

Take red (Mars), yellow (Venus) and green (Moon): When you drive your car these color symbols tell you when to stop (red-danger), wait (yellow-balance) and go (green-grow). Or, take a look at your electrical appliances, the television, radio, etc. To turn them on you dial to the right (Sun-positive), and to shut them off you switch to the left (Moon-negative). Light switches go up (Sun-positive) to turn on the current, and down (Moon-negative) to turn it off. Did you ever notice to which side a coat is buttoned? Men (Sun-male) button them to the right, and women (Moon-female) to the left. Volumes of common examples such as these could be cited. And the more one studies symbolism the more he is aware of the fascinating interlocking of objects in the environment by which he is habitually surrounded.

Learning to associate ideas with symbols will help you to develop your Extra Sensory Perception (ESP). And just as with any other helpful ability, increased ESP will aid you in many unthought-of ways. For example, when you misplace something or forget something you were supposed to do, ESP can give you the answer. ESP ability transfers to other areas in life in such a way that we are able to stamp out some of the confusion and uncertainty we often endure.

A professional artist deals with symbolical concepts, and a study of the tarot will give him an entirely different slant to his creativity. This also holds true for the musician and poet, who deal in emotions. Through a better understanding of symbolism, the art lover will gain a broader and deeper appreciation from any forms of art.

Students of spiritual philosophy or the beginner, aspiring to become an expert, gain amazing enlightenment from this book. Futhermore, gleaning a complete knowledge of any spiritual or sacred book, including the Bible, is only possible when the tarot interpretations of kabalistical meanings are understood. The tarot pictures appearing on the 22 Major Arcana provide fruitful subjects upon which to concentrate during periods of meditation. Associations undreamed of are revealed. Astrology and the tarot combined in their symbolism reveal keys to the secrets which were held for centuries within the confines of closed mystical brotherhoods for fear they would fall into the wrong hands.

This one-of-a-kind book takes a prominent place on the library shelf of the taroist, astrologer, mystic and layman. Its up-to-the-minute classifications earmark its effectiveness in dealing with today's problems in all phases of life.

Anyone, mystical student or not, can benefit from this book. By a simple application of the 1-2-3 steps given in this book, it will be possible for you to make an amazing beneficial transformation in your personality.

Becoming a good tarot card reader keeps you "on your toes"

and develops within you a high degree of mental alacrity, a "plus" factor which can be added to any area in your life—alertness on the job, keenness for study, and quick response to guide your children, to say nothing of the harmonious exchange you can enjoy with your mate.

Once the word gets around that you have the knack of reading the cards, people will want to meet you and know you better so that you can spread the cards for them. There are so many lonely people today, even in the middle of our bustling cities, to whom you could give a word of cheer and encouragement. A card-reading gift also allows you to read for your favorite club or pet charity. Furthermore, this talent could open doors to circles you have yearned to enter, making it possible for you to find new, influential friends who will help you to get what you want out of life.

CONTENTS

Contents

INTRODUCTION

If you are one of those people who smirk at the idea that square pasteboards bearing odd-looking hieroglyphics can tell you anything about your past, present or future, you are in for a big surprise. The Tarot Cards can do exactly that.

Impossible? So was the atomic bomb until its fantastic potency shocked an unbelieving world. Television, round-the-world jet flights, and moon shots were also labeled as impossible.

Idle tarot cards and untapped inner laws of nature are as useless as an unsplit atom. But like atomic energy directed into constructive endeavor, when the cards are employed to apply the laws of nature to your character development or problem solving, their released potential mushrooms into great benefits to you.

It is not necessary to believe in the tarot cards for them to work; nor do they have to be taken on faith. Experimentation will prove the point. We, ourselves, did not take them for granted when we started. We tabulated spreads and found results high above any chance average. Being down-to-earth, we were not interested in adopting a system which would not consistently reveal practical and helpful information.

Although the tarot may be new to you, it is almost as old as man himself. The Book of Thoth, or the tarot, was known to remotest antiquity. However, the spiritual science it expounded went "underground" for many centuries.

Ancient ruins give testimony of considerable scientific achievement long before history began. And even though modern man outpasses the ancients in physical science, he lags far behind in spiritual progress. These ruins and tradition tell of an ancient spiritual philosophy which transcends the reach of that known and practiced by the majority of people on earth today.

Through the centuries, science has replaced surmise with observed facts, and as a result of generations of progress, man has learned to protect himself from thousands of dangers that threaten his physical survival.

Due to such physically-oriented research, people have been prejudicially blocked from making a candid investigation of the spiritual facts of life. Therefore, *a spiritual decay is attacking man* because the very necessities of his human soul demand a knowledge which he is not developing.

To gain such knowledge, he should use the same strict methods of the physical scientists. Nebulous notions and uncertain surmise must be replaced by a framework of strict logic. Then man will be able to discover effective means of protecting himself when he is threatened on any plane—physical, emotional, mental or spiritual.

To build such a spiritual science demands the use of the *psychic senses*. Because the psychic senses, or astral senses, sometimes report falsely, they should be checked for accuracy by the physical senses. This was the manner in which the Ancient Masons marked every discovery of importance to the development and needs of the soul. Generation after generation, they specialized in two things: astrology, and gaining information concerning the soul of man. They developed their psychic senses to a high degree and laboriously kept records of their experiments for some 1,500 years. This record is called the Anu-Enlil Series of Chaldea and can be found in the British Museum of Natural History.

Astrology to them was not merely a means of character reading or predicting events, it was the science of the soul and the *key to all possibilities*. Each of their discoveries was marked with an appropriate symbol, and its esoteric interpretation was pictorially engraved on a separate tablet. The Egyptians called these tablets the Royal Road of Life. Their symbolism marks the Egyptian Tarot Cards.

Everything from a single thought to the evolution of a Solar System operates strictly upon numerical law. Both astrology and the tarot conform to mathematical principles as will be explained later. The Pyramid of Gizeh, built by these ancient magi to perpetuate early wisdom, still stands today. It is monumental proof of the relations existing between earth, the universe, and the soul of man.

As time goes on, modern discoveries concerning the Great Pyramid reaffirm ancient occult law. The Pyramid faces east and sits precisely in the center of the Northern Hemisphere, implying that the builders were aware even at that date of the oblate shape of the earth. Its physical measurements have been the subject of many books and articles correlating them with prophecy and symbolical conceptions. As mankind evolves, still more of the mysteries of the Pyramid will be revealed and substantiated.

Many examples might be presented to show an early knowledge of the tarot. As this subject has been handled effectively in kabalistical studies, repetition here is unnecessary. A scant reference to these various books soon reveals that later writings of early peoples showed less familiarity with the tarot as time went on.

The Prophets Ezekiel and Daniel show some knowledge of it, and *certainly whoever wrote the Apocalypse based it all upon the tarot.* Each of its 22 chapters deals with the 22 Major Arcana of the Tarot as applied to prophecy. It is doubtful that a complete knowledge of any sacred book, including the Bible, can be fully understood by one who knows nothing of the tarot which allows the interpretation of the so-called mysteries of the kabala. Yet to manipulate the tarot, which is the Silver Key, one needs the Golden Key of Astrology.

From time to time, archaeologists discover remnants of

these two keys all over the world. For instance, in 1964 the greatest excavation of its kind in recent history and one of the most important archaeological finds of the 20th century took place in Egypt. The famed "Avenue of the Sphinxes," described in Egyptian history as linking the temples of Luxor and Karnak, was being unearthed by removing 3,000 years of debris and dust.

Egyptologists estimate that the 20-foot wide, stone road is two miles long and lined by 1,400 sphinxes, 700 on each side spaced 15 feet apart. The sphinxes, which are 10 feet long and 4 feet high, were built by many pharaohs between 1200 B.C. and 378 B.C. Inscriptions and hieroglyphics adorn each 5-foot high stone base.

Hermetic tradition holds that a yet-uncovered record of the two keys—astrology and the tarot—is to be found inside of the Great Pyramid. It tells of a tunnel leading through and under the paws of the Sphinx to an Egyptian Initiation Temple. In this temple along the walls are the tablets mentioned above upon which are inscribed the tarot cards depicting the story of the soul's initiation as it travels the Cycle of Necessity.

There are 108 tablets; 78 of them are what we know as the exoteric tarot, and 30 of them are the esoteric tarot. T. H. Burgoyne, a Brotherhood of Light initiate, in his *Light of Egypt* describes the esoteric pictures under the caption "The Tablets of Aeth." But to our knowledge these tablets have never been produced on the physical plane.

The late C. C. Zain, a modern Brotherhood of Light initiate and founder of the Church of Light, presented the exoteric deck of Tarot Cards in his book *The Sacred Tarot*, which has become the most comprehensive reference work on the subject to date. His Hermetic System of the Kabala is the foundation for this volume.

Through the kind permission of The Church of Light at Los Angeles, we present here the illustrations of the Egyptian

Tarot Cards. They were painstakingly designed, correct in all details, from a description of the figures on the walls of the Egyptian Initiation Chamber from the originals preserved on the inner planes.

Zain writes: "The Egyptian Tarot pictures . . . teach in still greater detail the same spiritual ideas that are taught by the constellations. Both constellations in the sky . . . and the Tarot pictures adorning the walls of the ancient Egyptian Initiation Chamber, make use of primitive symbolical pictograph writing to convey the most important things the ancient wise ones found out about the human soul. The Egyptian Tarot, then, portrays the spiritual conceptions of the Egyptian initiates, as derived from a still more remote past [from Atlantis and Mu]. There is a peculiar sympathy, however, between the thoughts of man and actions for which he finds no rational motive. That is, the same sympathy which exits between the happenings on earth and the positions of the planets in the sky also manifests through the unconscious mind.

"If we but analyze our dreams we shall find that symbolism is the common language of the unconscious mind. And the successful use of the tarot cards as instruments of divination depends upon their sympathetic response to invisible factors of intelligence. So it would be indeed strange if they responded merely in the transitory laying of the spread, and not also in their symbolism to the minds of those who handle them."

But some of the fragments filtered through to the public in a vague and disconnected manner. The profane and ignorant of occult law pounced upon these fragments and used them for their own personal gain to enslave others. What they gave out distorted the true import of the ancient symbolism. This trend also had a marked influence on the varying presentations of cards which then proved ineffective to help a neophyte become adept, because the basic vibratory influences were false.

When people of a different conception of life handled the cards, they naturally changed the pictures on them to portray their own strong convictions and to depict the environment in which they lived at the time. Their approach was purely materialistic.

A cogent analogy is seen in the Knight (Horseman) of Swords at the beginning of the Christian era. It shows an armored crusader, dashing across the frontier into another's domain in the well-known effort to spread enlightenment by means of the sword. The picture suggests instantly the conquest of far-flung empires and the forceful dissemination of Christian creeds among the benighted heathens thus conquered.

In a similar manner many decks came into existence, each pack being unconsciously modified by the philosophy of the life of the group using them. Even the common playing cards we know today are derived from the ancient tarot and vary widely due to their centuries of use as instruments of gambling.

Because of inherent characteristics, the English, German, Italian, French and Gypsy cards differ. Yet because each is altered to align with their deep convictions, each group uses them successfully for fortune telling due to the sympathetic response between the cards and their subconscious minds.

Commonly occult historians place the earliest record of tarot cards back in the 14th century. Yet Hermetic tradition holds them to be about 35,000 years old. The decks which evolved in preceding centuries were not keyed to the authentic associations with universal law as researched by the ancient magi. There was good reason for this descrepancy.

When the dogmatic priesthood took over, the knowledge went underground. Man had not evolved to a level where he could understand the spiritual significance behind the symbolism, nor had he learned to control the forces that surround him on both the physical and astral plane. Dealing with occult energies is dangerous unless one knows what he is doing.

Custodians of this spiritual knowledge were forced to keep the information within the confines of secret brotherhoods where the members went through a rigorous spiritual training before the truths were revealed to them. In this manner, the mysteries were divulged to candidates only after they had surmounted trials and hardships to prove their worthiness.

In this Aquarian Age astronauts are probing outer-space, and aquanauts are exploring the ocean-depths. Man has evolved to a high physical level, and he has access to the widest of educational facilities. This is a fantastic era for man to investigate anything and everything about himself and the universe.

Take the tarot cards. We urge you to utilize the splendid opportunity for investigation that reading them provides. From the standpoint of personal development, you can employ the cards to speed your own progress or that of anyone for whom you read.

With a minimum of study, practice and personal investigation, you will undoubtedly find that the application of tarot reading could bring you a lifting of the spirit, a new and better way of life, or your own heart's desire.

FUNCTIONS OF THE TAROT

𝒯 he Sacred Tarot sprang from the need to record ideas in universal symbolism. And these recorded ideas, embraced in the tarot, can be applied in four different ways as:

1. A Science of Vibration
2. A Spiritual Science
3. A System of Divination by Cards
4. A System of Divination by Numbers

To understand the application of the tarot, it is important to keep these four functions separate so that one will not become confused with the other. Each function is in itself a definite and clear-cut system, standing apart from the other three.

Two of these systems—Science of Vibration and Spiritual Science—are positive and therefore scientific in nature. Because of their electric, masculine nature, these systems are based on the esoteric principles of life. Numbers furnish the key to the Science of Vibration; and the Spiritual Science forms the basis of a complete philosophy of life.

The other two systems are negative and therefore divinatory in nature. They are a system of Divination by Cards, and a system of Divination by Numbers. Because of their magnetic, feminine nature, these systems are based on the exoteric principles of life.

These four functions correspond to the Jod-He-Vau-He, which is the magical quaternary representing a formula found to be valuable in the solution of all problems.

Magical Quarternary

	Sign	*Triplicity*	*Tarot Function*
Jod	Leo	Fire	Science of Vibration
He	Scorpio	Water	Divination by Cards
Vau	Taurus	Earth	Divination by Numbers
He	Aquarius	Air	Spiritual Science

This book focuses the attention on the first He in the table above, which is Divination by Cards, that is, reading tarot-card spreads. Although the other three functions are mentioned or implied, they are not thoroughly explored here. However, the information gained from the study of the correspondences in this book may easily be translated into applicable terms which will help in the study of the other three functions.

The primary reason for selecting Divination by Cards as the subject matter of this book was the insistent need for it. Many authorities throughout the years have expounded and thoroughly explored the other three functions. But, to our knowledge, the demonstration and reading of various types of spreads has never been adequately covered.

We have selected The Egyptian Tarot Cards, because they embrace more symbolical factors than are found on any other deck, and these symbols are based upon correct numerical and astrological correspondences. This, in itself, lifts these cards out of the realm of mere fortune telling and aligns them with universal principles.

The tarot bears the same relation to astrology as the moon bears to the sun. It is the sun that brings us the light of day; and astrology brings radiant light upon the more evident truths of our philosophy in daily living. However, the elusive mysteries, which seem to be hidden from view by the material rush of living, are buried deep—dark as the night, until the moon reflects the light of the sun.

The moon borrows her light from the sun, and the tarot bears this same relationship by borrowing significance from astrology. Light can be shed upon the darkest mental pathways. Therefore, the two keys—astrology and the tarot—in the hands of an efficient tarot-card reader unlock the secrets of nature's apparent mysteries.

HOW THE TAROT CARDS WORK

Few of the motions we make result from premeditated thought. They are directed by the subconsious mind. Take walking, for instance. It is true that we think of walking and then walk. But we certainly do not center our attention on the complex and intricate process of balancing the action of one muscle against another. Rather, our nervous systems have been educated to respond immediately to the orders given by our subconscious minds.

Since the subconscious mind is familiar with this "causing of unconscious muscular activity," it is easier for it to communicate intelligent thoughts by directing muscular actions than by impressing the physical brain directly. Therefore, under ordinary circumstances, using unconscious muscular activity is the easiest method possible for the communication of what is in the subconscious to the physical brain.

The range of subconscious perception is far greater than that of the physical senses. All that a person has ever experienced or known is stored in his subconscious. It may also contact almost any imaginable source of information beyond that which has been stored by the individual.

As soon as the subconscious mind focuses its attention on obtaining specific information, the psychic senses respond with alacrity. They are able, due to their wider range of perception, to acquire information inaccessible to physical senses. This information resides as a memory in the subconscious.

Therefore, before laying a spread of tarot cards, it is important to ask a definite question. This focuses the attention of the subconscious on obtaining the information wanted. Then as the cards are shuffled, cut and dealt, concentrating on the question adds energy which the subconscious can use in gathering pertinent facts.

In addition, the tarot cards also act as a means of directing the subconscious to aquire such information. An experienced reader feels the presence of a power. This power not only directs how the cards shall be read, but actually determines the way they fall so that a correct reading will result. Other forces may be brought into play, but the most significant factor influencing the proper distribution of the cards into a spread is the unconscious muscular activity of the arms and hands.

The accuracy of the information received depends upon the ability of the reader's subconscious to perceive conditions not known to the objective consciousness and bring it through. To do this requires electromagnetic energy. Manipulating the tarot cards requires the use of extrasensory perception and psychokinetic power.

CONTENTS AND ARRANGEMENT

Information necessary to learn the art of laying and reading spreads is presented in four parts. Reviewing the introductory material to each section is vitally essential.

PART I presents a detailed explanation of how to care for and use the cards properly. This information should be read completely, for applying it will help to avoid a long and tedious apprenticeship.

PART II gives instructions and diagrams of diversified, easy-to-read spreads. They demonstrate how fourteen actual life questions dealing with the past, present and future can be read. In some instances the result of what happened when the counsel of the reader was applied is noted, and in others the reading projects itself far into the future.

PART III explains the basic symbolical patterns of each card, touches on universal symbolism and contains a ready-reference list of key phrases for each one of the cards.

PART IV is a compendium of astrological rulerships—signs and planets—to help broaden the scope of the meaning symbolized by each card.

Part J

YOUR ZAROZ CARDS AND HOW ZO USE ZHEM

*U*nderstanding the principle of radiation is our first consideration in effectively handling and reading the tarot cards. Every thing and every person *radiates*. The magnetism and thought emanations of people impart qualities in inanimate objects such as the tarot cards.

To obtain optimum results, do not allow anyone to handle your tarot cards except when shuffling and cutting before a reading. The more you, yourself, handle the cards, the more gratifying your results will be. This handling impregnates the cards with your own personal magnetism, forming a rapport between your subconscious and the cards—an association which becomes stronger as you continue to use your cards.

Recognizing this rapport makes it easy to see why new cards are not as responsive as a deck which has been used for a long time by a reader. You, as a new card reader, should be aware of this fact. Then you will not feel discouraged with your first attempts at reading spreads.

Care of the Cards

Special care of your cards is needed to protect them from unwanted vibrations. Never leave them lying around the house. And you should not place them near things that are often used by other people. If you do, you will invite a mixture of vibrations which will tend to confuse your reading. Keep them somewhere away from discordant vibrations. This place should be near your own things having your own personal vibrations in them.

Because of the subtle absorption of vibrations, your cards should be stored in a wooden box. It need not be large, but perhaps large enough to hold two decks of cards. Commonly, one deck is used for spiritual enlightenment and the other for material questions. A white pine box serves splendidly. When the cards are kept in this box, their vibrations are sealed in. Furthermore, due to the high non-conductibility of the wood, they are protected from undesirable vibrations.

Before placing the cards in the box, wrap them in a colored piece of silk corresponding to the best sign or the best planet in your own horoscope. If you do not know your best sign or planet, select a color that stimulates you harmoniously.

Signs and Tarot Color Correspondences

Aries	light red	Libra	light yellow
Taurus	dark yellow	Scorpio	dark red
Gemini	light violet	Sagittarius	light purple
Cancer	green	Capricorn	dark blue
Leo	orange	Aquarius	light blue
Virgo	dark violet	Pisces	dark purple

Planets and Tarot Color Correspondences

Sun	orange	Jupiter	purple
Moon	green	Saturn	blue
Mercury	violet	Uranus	dazzling white
Venus	yellow	Neptune	iridescence
Mars	red	Pluto	ultraviolet

Using your best color will furnish you with an opportunity to stimulate the most harmonious center within your mind, thus adding to the pleasure and effectiveness you will obtain from handling your cards.

Where to Read the Cards

Our next consideration is where to spread the cards. Any flat surface, such as a table, will do. If possible, it is best to have a special table or a tarot board constructed of soft, white pine.

The surface should be big enough to accommodate the largest spread. It should be unvarnished and unpainted so that it will become impregnated with the vibrations of the reader. By using this surface for tarot readings exclusively, extraneous thought-vibrations will not interfere with the reading. This will insure the ideal condition for the manifestation of inner-plane intelligences.

The reading environment is equal in importance to the tarot board. When a reader is forced to work in a place where there has been a violent fight, for example, the discordant vibrations bring a static condition to the special type of psychic rapport required. These lower vibrations, resulting from a quarrel, attract lower entities who interfere with the unconscious minds of both the reader and client.

To prevent this static condition, both reader and client should strongly direct their thoughts and feelings to a higher level. However, maintaining this level is difficult in an animalistic environment, and the energy used could be better spent on the reading itself. It is true that after one becomes proficient in the art of reading the tarot cards, if he is forced to, he can read in almost any environment. Still, the ideal conditions will be found in a place where peaceful vibrations exist.

In addition to this, just before and during the reading there should be no small talk. The attention should not be allowed to stray to anything except the business at hand. In this concentrated vibration, the law of affinity works unhindered, helping both reader and client keep a definite thought-attraction. When this thought-attraction is firmly established, the cards will fall in such a way as to give a definite answer to the question.

The querent, or person asking the question, should sit opposite the reader. If a tarot board is used, it may rest upon their knees or on a table. And because the natural magnetic currents of the earth flow from north to south, the reader should be facing north and the querent facing south. Taking these positions allows the two to build a relationship of positive to negative.

When the querent is absent, it is also possible to read the cards for him. Then you both shuffle and read the cards yourself. In this case, or if you are reading the cards for yourself, face the east—the source of light. In either case, after taking the appropriate positions, the deck is placed on a surface in front of the reader.

Preparation for Reading

Before touching the cards, the reader should impress the querent with the necessity of a serious attitude—joking, banter and small talk detract from the vibration and affect the spread. All desires and thoughts aside from the question should be cleared from both minds.

Next should be discussed precisely what information is desired. Usually this has to be clarified, because questions are often asked incorrectly. The reader should encourage the client to talk about his problem. Then a background view of his past circumstances which led up to the present problem will be revealed. Knowing something of the client's conditioning will assist the reader to select the proper key phrase for each card.

Selecting the Spread

As the reader listens to the background story, he will be impressed to select the type of spread which will best answer the client's question. Questions asked fall into three broad categories: (1) personal questions, (2) mundane questions of public interest, and (3) spiritual questions. As a rule, most questions may be answered by employing any spread. However, certain subject matter usually lends itself more easily to specific spreads.

For instance, if the simple Yes or No Spread will answer the question, select it. However, a complex problem demands a more embracive spread, such as the Life Spread or the Spread of 36. If periods of time extending far into the future are involved, then the Pyramid Spread or the Solar Spread may be used.

Sample Questions and Selected Spreads

Questions	Suggested Spreads
1. Personal Questions:	
Does so-and-so love me?	Yes or No Spread
	Magic Seven Spread
What steps should I take	Sephiroth Spread
to improve my business?	Kabala Spread
I wish I could increase my	Wish Spread
earning power.	Magic Seven Spread
	Horoscope Spread
What can I do to help	Spread of 36
make my son's future a	Solar Spread
success?	
2. Public Interest Questions:	
Will so-and-so be elected	Pyramid Spread
U.S. President?	Yes or No Spread
Will the tax-cut bill be	Yes or No Spread
passed by Congress?	Magic Seven Spread
	Magic Cross Spread

| Will the kidnappers be caught? | Yes or No Spread
Wish Spread |

3. Spiritual Questions:

What can I do to improve my character?	Magic Seven Spread Magic Cross Spread
What is my cosmic mission?	Three Sevens Spread Life Spread
Am I mentally prepared for astral travel ?	Kabala Spread Magic Cross Spread

Training the Subconscious

At this point it seems advisable to mention to the tarot card reader the importance of training the subconscious mind. Being plastic, the subconscious bends to each new thought or idea presented to it. Therefore, to focus it requires control. So the subconscious should be impressed with what to expect. Then the required rapport will result if orders are given firmly and backed up with will power.

A systematic approach allows the subconscious to know what is expected of it. This approach is based upon clearly defining the question, selecting an appropriate spread, and shuffling and cutting the cards in the same manner each time.

These steps aid the mind and any psychic intelligence that may be present to know exactly how the cards will be handled. And through the intra-muscular activity, the mind and these intelligences will be alerted to make the proper arrangement of cards leading to a more accurate reading. It should be remembered that the subconscious never asks why, it merely follows orders.

Because the subconscious is bombarded at all times with multiple stimulation, both physical and mental, spontaneous attention and fantasy thinking too easily disrupt or alter thought patterns. Therefore, the mind should be trained in the art of directed thinking and induced emotion. This must be done so that the mind will not tune in on irrelevant material.

Shuffling and Cutting

To control the direction of thought and the resultant intramuscular activity, both the reader and the querent concentrate on the question. They hold the thought that truth will be revealed no matter what the querent would like the outcome to be. Then the reader hands the cards to the querent, asking him to shuffle and cut them three times.

The cards are shuffled once and then cut into three packs. These packs are then gathered into one pack. This procedure is performed three times. After shuffling and cutting, the querent hands the cards to the reader and does not touch them again.

The decision of how the cards are actually shuffled depends on personal preference since the method employed is of little importance. To manipulate a large deck of seventy-eight cards demands no small amount of dexterity. For this reason, many find that the overhand shuffle is accomplished with more comfort than the riffle shuffle. And to further facilitate ease in shuffling, the cards may be turned the long way and overhand shuffled.

But no matter which shuffle is selected, it is advisable to stick to the one which is easiest. Then the mechanics of shuffling will not distract, allowing the attention to be focused on the question.

Some of the cards should be reversed in the process of shuffling or cutting. This may be done as intuition prompts or in a pre-established pattern.

Spreading the Cards

The right hand is positive like the Sun, and the left hand is negative like the Moon. So to crystallize the magnetic flow of this positive to negative current, the cards are dealt from right to left, unless specific patterns are used. In these cases, the cards are dealt in the sequence in which they will be read. The reader lays the cards face down one at a time in the previously decided upon spread. The reader then sets aside the cards not used.

Reading the Cards

The cards are always viewed from the reader's position. This is important when considering the reversed position of a card. The cards are always turned over from top to bottom, one at a time as read, following the pattern given in the instructions. This prevents the mind from wandering to other cards in the spread, allowing directed thought to be given to each individual card.

A card right end up is slightly more fortunate than its common significance, similar to a planet in a horoscope receiving a slightly harmonious aspect.

A card wrong end up, or reversed, is slightly less fortunate than its common significance, similar to a planet in a horoscope receiving a slightly discordant aspect.

When each card is turned, it is considered as an event or influence following the last card read. In this way, a continuity is kept from beginning to end as the reading progresses from one card to another.

In several of the spread diagrams in PART II, EXAMPLE TAROT CARD READINGS, Key Cards are used. These Key Cards usually designate divisions of time, such as past, present, or future. If a Major Arcanum falls on a Key Card station, the period it represents is strongly involved with the topic matter of the spread.

Finally, it should be remembered that the scope of a reading is always limited by the present circumstances and past conditioning of the querent.

With the basic principles of the care and use of your cards firmly set in your mind, you are now ready to undertake the fascinating activity of reading tarot spreads.

Part II

EXAMPLE TAROT
CARD READINGS

$\mathcal{F}$ or those well versed
in the language of the tarot cards, this section needs no explanation. However, to those who are new at reading tarot spreads, we offer a suggestion. Before proceeding, first read PART I which will clarify basic factors and bring more meaning to these spreads.

To lend interest to the demonstration of how tarot cards are read in a spread, we have selected questions dealing with actual life problems rather than imaginary ones. We feel that the choice will have a wide appeal to the general public, and that these questions may be ones which you, yourself, have asked at one time or another.

In order to derive the most information from the symbolism on each card, we suggest that you lay out the demonstrated spreads using your own cards. Then watch you own cards as you follow the given reading. In addition to capturing the symbolism, you will quickly learn the origin of each key phrase. You will be impregnating the cards with your vibrations before you attempt to make spreads of your own. This will narrow down your chances of making poor spreads and help to avoid a feeling of discouragement.

This section includes fourteen readings. The how-to-do-it presentation is the same for all of them. First comes the instructions of how to make the spread itself, accompanied with a diagram of the sequence of how to lay out the cards. When you start making your own personal spreads, you will refer to these instructions many times.

In each instance, motivation is summed up by an actual life story or circumstance, which leads to the question asked. This is accompanied by the actual spread resulting when the cards were shuffled, cut and spread for the question. Numbers appearing outside the cards in the spread indicate the reading sequence, and an R inside the card, indicates a card which is reversed in position.

With this is reading of the spread which varies slightly in its form due to the nature of the spread. All words in italics are taken from PART III, KEY PHRASES. Only verb tenses and personal pronouns are changed from time to time to fit the reading, but the key phrase remains essentially the same.

The reader's intuition, stimulated by the symbolic keys, should be relied upon when reading his own spreads. The key phrases given here are merely guides. However, we have confined ourselves to these key phrases to demonstrate how they can be used under any given circumstance.

I. YES OR NO SPREAD

Should you want a quick yes or no answer to a question, this spread will serve your purpose. Five, seven, or nine cards may be used, depending upon the amount of detail desired.

Regardless of the number of cards used, the middle card (Key Card) counts two and each other card counts one. When the majority of counts are right end up, the answer is yes; but if the majority are reversed, the answer is no. Should the number of counts be evenly divided, no definite yes or no answer is indicated.

There are several conditions which prompt the counts to fall evenly divided between yes and no; lack of concentration on the question while shuffling and cutting; not a strong enough desire to know the answer; wishing for what you want rather than the truth; or undecided factors associated with the topic matter.

Sometimes a mere yes or no answer is all that is required, but if details are desired, the Key Card is read as the *present*. The cards to the right represent conditions or events of the *past* leading up to the present. And the cards to the left of the Key Card indicate the *future* of the matter.

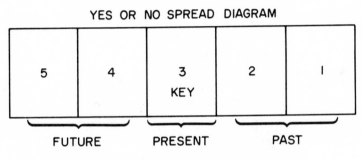

YES OR NO SPREAD DIAGRAM

Yes or No Spread Demonstrated

A bachelor who lived in an apartment was constantly bothered by his neighbor—a married woman. She would join his parties uninvited, bring him gifts, and borrow household items at all hours of the day and night. While her husband was away at work, she often found excuses to invite the bachelor in—to watch television or to fix her household appliances. She would take these opportunities to tell of her husband's jealous nature.

After sizing up the situation, the bachelor cut off the relationship by avoiding her. As time went on the situation became uncomfortable for him, because he was basically friendly and found it difficult to avoid her. Furthermore, he felt embarrassed whenever he saw her husband.

This embarrassment prompted him to ask the question: "Will my neighbor move within the next six months?"

After the cards were shuffled and dealt in the designated manner, they fell in the following pattern.

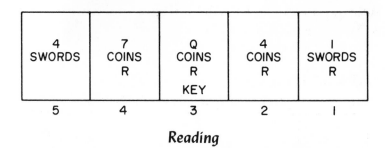

4 SWORDS	7 COINS R	Q COINS R KEY	4 COINS R	I SWORDS R
5	4	3	2	I

Reading

Cards number 1, 2, 3 and 4 are reversed, giving five no's. Card number 5, being right end up, designates one yes. Therefore, the answer to the question is: no, the neighbor will not move within the next six months.

Past

The bachelor had (1) *difficulty in adjustment* due to differences in personalities, and although he received a (2) *gift from a friend* there was too much infringement upon his privacy.

Present

The bachelor is represented by the (3) Queen of Coins (reversed), indicating a *man of a Libra temperament.*

Future

(4) *Directed mental energy solves a problem* by bachelor not allowing neighbor to upset him. And he can (5) *win through more give and take.*

The querent (bachelor) was advised to solve his problem by using his mind instead of his emotions. He was told to establish a relationship of an impersonal nature with his neighbor.

As she was not going to move, he made a constructive effort to relieve his uncomfortable state. Over a year later the neighbor had still not moved, and the bachelor had adjusted to the situation.

2. PYRAMID SPREAD

This versatile spread may be used to: (1) answer a question, (2) solve a problem, or (3) show the general trend of events as they may be expected in a person's life.

Shuffle and cut the cards in the usual manner. Then deal 21 cards face downward, dealing from right to left until the top of the pyramid is reached as indicated by the diagram.

To understand the reading sequence, note that each Key Card is also considered as the first card of the next group of five. The four cards just to the right of a Key Card represent past events leading up to the time represented by that Key Card. A Key Card is always significant, but if a Major Arcanum appears on a Key Card station, the period of time it represents takes on greater importance.

In this spread there are five Key Cards:

Key I   Present
Key II   Immediate Future
Key III   Next Turn of Events
Key IV   Distant Future
Key V   End of the Matter

Pyramid Spread Demonstrated

A middle-aged widow who lived near the seashore suffered from a chronic chest condition. Her discordant reactions to the people in her life caused increasing emotional tensions which contributed to her chest attacks.

When her doctor advised her to move away from the fog, she arranged to sell her beach home and purchase a home in

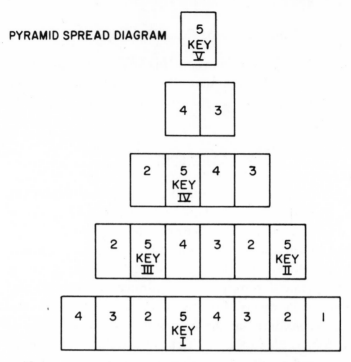

the desert. Because of her lack of physical strength and the fact that the desert home was located in a sparsely populated area, it was necessary for her to find someone to live there with her. Even though she made arrangements for a lady companion to accompany her, she was still worried. She wondered if her companion would like the quiet desert life well enough to be willing to stay on with her.

Her deep concern prompted her to ask the question: "Will I be able to make a permanent home in the desert?" The cards were set up in the spread accompanying the reading analysis.

Reading

As the outcome of this spread is known, the subsequent events will be interspersed in the reading of the cards.

Present

Counting five cards from the right on the bottom row brings us to the Present, Key İ. Here we find reversed Major Arcanum XIV, signifying that the querent is not *keeping*

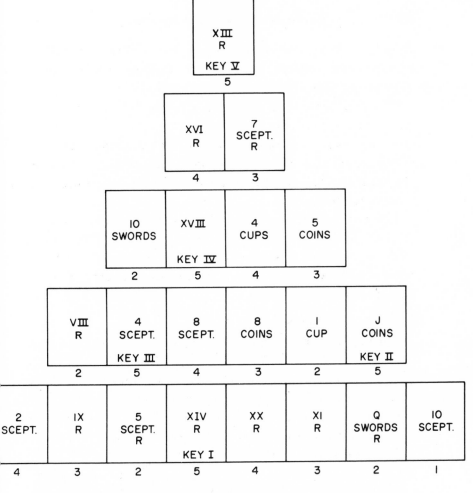

company with harmonious people. This shows her desire to escape from an unhappy environment.

The first card, representing the distant past, is the Ten of Scepters—*the new replaces the old.* This past trend was reflected in a complete change in her life upon the death of a friend who lived with her.

The next card to the left is the reversed Queen of Scepters, representing *a man of a Virgo temperament.* This refers to a man who contested the dead friend's will without success. The querent was named as sole beneficiary. While the legal aspects were being worked out, she suffered much indecision as to how to handle her inherited money. Her co-workers, mostly women, offered her all kinds of advice, and criticized (Virgo) her plans.

The third card from the right is reversed Major Arcanum XI—*confusion and lack of force.* As time went on, her health problems increased, and the discordant emotional reactions to the unsolicited advice led to her unhappy state of mind. She couldn't make a decision about anything and almost had a nervous breakdown.

The fourth card from the right, just before the Present, is reversed Major Arcanum XX—*passing of an old condition leads to a new one.* She sold her beach home and bought a desert home. As both homes went into escrow, her apprehension increased.

Immediate Future

Starting with Key I and counting ahead five cards brings us to the right-hand card of the second row. This Key II represents the Immediate Future. Here we find the Jack of Coins—*a man of an Aquarian temperament.*

Leading up to this is the Five of Scepters—*good fortune in business.* This card indicates the time she received the escrow papers. When she signed them, she felt a measure of relief, because now it seemed as if her dream was finally coming true.

Then comes Major Arcanum IX—*actions influenced by environment.* When she received the final escrow papers, she was upset because they differed from the original ones. As she was being charged for two years back taxes, she went to her bank to seek advice. They advised her not to sign.

The next card is the Two of Scepters—*obstacles resolved through analysis.* She took a special trip to the desert town where the papers were filed and was informed that the tax clause would be deleted.

This brings us back to Key II, the *Aquarian man,* who brought the final escrow papers to her. Having gained a clear title to the property, she was immensely relieved.

Next Turn of Events

Starting with Key II and counting ahead five cards, brings us to Key III, representing the Next Turn of Events. It is the Four of Scepters—*a successful enterprise*. And that is what it appeared to be.

Leading up to this is the Ace of Cups—*travel concerned with domestic affairs*. After receiving the final escrow papers, she and her companion moved to the desert with their belongings.

The next card is the Eight of Coins—*compatible partnership*. The companion was enthusiastic about getting the new home settled. This pleased the querent, because her health prevented her from doing strenuous work.

The following card is the Eight of Scepters—*rely on your own judgment*. After her companion had the furniture arranged and the house in order, she soon became bored and restless. So the querent, who found her companion likeable, decided to try to make her life more attractive. They drove out for dinner several evenings a week investigating the restaurants in nearby towns.

This brings us to Key III, the Four of Scepters. The companion brightened up and seemed happier, and it began to look as though the move to the desert had turned out to be *a successful enterprise*.

Distant Future

Starting with Key III and counting ahead five cards brings us to Key IV representing the Distant Future. It is Major Arcanum XVIII—*energetic action overcomes lethargy*.

Leading up to this is reversed Major Arcanum VIII—*develop a spirit of give and take*. The querent became worried when she noticed that her companion was becoming restless again. Again she took extra pains to make her companion more contented.

The next card is the Five of Coins—*a trip for achievement*.

Afraid that her companion would not remain with her, the querent took her to see various interesting desert spots. Being ill, this extra activity taxed her energy tremendously, but she was determined to keep the companion with her at all cost.

Next falls the Four of Cups—*pleasure in group activity*. For a time the desert jaunts were enough to hold the interest of the companion. However, as soon as the limited list was exhausted, she once more became bored. At the suggestion of the querent, the companion invited some of her friends out for a week. All that week, the companion was the happiest person in the world.

This brings us back to Key IV which reads *energetic action overcomes lethargy*. After her friends departed, the companion brooded. She hardly spoke at all and left her work undone. Eventually, the querent called the whole thing off, and they packed up and moved back to the coast, each going her separate way.

End of the Matter

Starting with Major Arcanum XVIII and counting ahead five cards brings us to the last card—Key V, representing the End of the Matter. It is Major Arcanum XIII—*end of a situation*.

Leading up to this is the Ten of Swords—*agitation upsets balance*. This was an extremely emotional period for the querent. She moved into a small, cramped place while looking for a new home, and felt remorse because her desert home had not worked out. As a result, she suffered another severe chest attack.

Then follows reversed Seven of Scepters—*benefit through professionals*. Her doctor (who treated her for her chest condition) put her in touch with a buyer for her desert home, and she sold it for cash.

The next card is reversed Major Arcanum XVI—*you reap what you sow*. As she had always been kind to the companion, even when the tension was highest, the companion agreed to return to her employ. The querent bought a home right next door to the one she had sold before she moved to the desert.

The final card at the top of the spread is Key V, representing the *end of a situation* (Major Arcanum XIII). She had come full circle, realizing that desert living was something she physically could not afford.

3. SEPHIROTH SPREAD

To do this spread, first remove the twenty-two Major Arcana and the four Aces from the deck. These twenty-six cards are the only ones used in the Sephiroth Spread.

The Four Aces

The Aces of Coins, Scepters, Cups, and Swords represent the four astral kingdoms. These Aces are called the Astral Keys because they key the entire spread and are, therefore, more potent than any of the other cards in the spread.

After shuffling and cutting the four Aces three times in the usual manner, they are dealt as illustrated in the diagram on page 48. The first Ace is dealt on the Kingdom marked Asc.; the second Ace on the M.C.; the third Ace on the Desc.; and the fourth Ace on the N.C.

These four stations, or Astral Kingdoms, are comparable to the four angles of a horoscope. Astrologically, Asc. stands for the Ascendant or first house; M.C. stands for Midheaven or tenth house; Desc. stands for Descendant or seventh house; and N.C. stands for Nadir or fourth house.

The Four Astral Kingdoms

The first Astral Kingdom, marked Asc., pertains to Life. The reading of the Kingdom is keyed to the suit of the Ace.

Ace of Coins—strength, vigor, vitality.
Ace of Scepters—favorable, denotes work and responsibility.
Ace of Cups—love of pleasure may deplete vitality.
Ace of Swords—sickness or death.

The second Astral Kingdom, marked M.C., is concerned with Honor and Business. The suit of the Ace determines the meaning of the Kingdom.

> Ace of Scepters—great power.
> Ace of Coins—favorable, much effort required.
> Ace of Cups—honor blemished through pursuing too much pleasure.
> Ace of Swords—failure.

The third Astral Kingdom, marked Desc., embraces Love or War. The Ace falling on this Kingdom indicates the reading.

> Ace of Cups—joy and happiness.
> Ace of Swords—disputes.
> Ace of Scepters—difficulties through difference in station.
> Ace of Coins—abundant strength.

The fourth Astral Kingdom, marked N.C., relates to Secret Things or Results. As with the other Kingdoms, interpretation is based upon the Ace which falls here.

> Ace of Swords—a favorable ending.
> Ace of Cups—pleasant results.
> Ace of Coins—unfortunate.
> Ace of Scepters—hard struggle, inadequate returns.

If the question for which the cards were spread relates to Life, begin the reading with the Asc. If the question has to do with Love or War, start with the Desc. If it concerns Honor or Business, commence with the M.C. Should the question deal with Secret Things or Results, begin the reading with the N.C.

The Twenty-Two Major Arcana

Consulting the diagram you will note that there are ten thrones, designated by the Roman Numerals. Each throne has two cards. The twenty-two Major Arcana are shuffled, cut, and then dealt around the ten thrones from I to X—placing one card on each throne as numbered. Then the rest of the cards are dealt back from throne X to throne I.

The two cards remaining are placed to the right of the spread. This station is called the staff, and it is consulted only if the reading seems contradictory. Then the two cards of the staff will reveal why a plain answer was not forthcoming.

Reading Sequence

The diagram shows the Asc. and Desc. having three thrones of two cards each; and the M.C. and N.C. having only two thrones of two cards each. These ten thrones are designated by Roman Numerals. In reading the Asc. or Desc., the two cards on the center thrones (I or VI), indicate the most important factors. The cards on the other four thrones (II and X or V and VII) signify modifying influences. The four cards on the thrones of the M.C. or N.C. are of equal importance.

Question: every question possible belongs to one of the four kingdoms. First locate the Ace, or astral key, of the question. Turn this Ace over, from top to bottom, noting its significance. Then turn over the cards belonging to its thrones. The cards on the thrones of the question will indicate why the conditions signified by the Ace shown there exist and give some details.

Opposition: next turn over the opposite Ace, which pictures the opposition to the matter. The cards on its thrones show details of this opposition.

Progress: the next kingdom read is the one which lies clockwise from the kingdom representing the question. This Ace, and the cards of its thrones, represent the progress of the matter.

End: the end of the matter is shown by the Ace opposing the progress. This Ace, and the cards on its throne, give the significance and details of the end of the matter.

Table of Reading Sequence

Subject Matter	Question	Opposition	Progress	End
Physical body, self interests, personality.	Asc.	Desc.	M.C.	N.C.
Marriage, love, enemies, war, partnerships.	Desc.	Asc.	N.C.	M.C.
Business, employment, honor, reputation.	M.C	N.C.	Desc.	Asc.
Hidden things, psychic matters, secrets.	N.C.	M.C.	Asc.	Desc.

SEPHIROTH SPREAD DIAGRAM

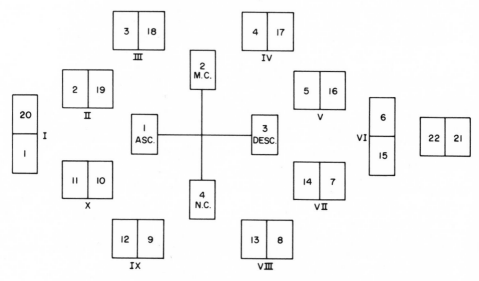

Sephiroth Spread Demonstrated

Being very much in love, a recently married couple had a strong desire to maintain a successful marriage. Each had brought heavy financial obligations to the union. Realizing that financial problems account for more divorces than any other single factor, they were deeply concerned.

But more than finances, in their sincerity, they were interested in all other departments of their lives as well. Futhermore, they wanted to be aware of any problem, which they could not consciously anticipate themselves, that might possibly threaten their marriage. In order to get an idea of future trends, they asked the question: "What can we do to make our marriage a success?"

The cards were shuffled and cut in the usual manner, and were dealt as indicated. They fell in the following pattern.

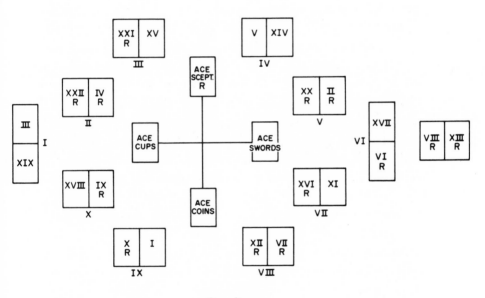

Reading

Because this is a question about marriage, the Desc. becomes the Question. The Desc. and its three thrones of two cards each represent the marriage. The Asc. and its three thrones of two cards each represent the Opposition to the success of the marriage. The N.C. with its two thrones of two cards each represent the Progress of the marriage. And the M.C. with its two thrones of two cards each indicate the culmination or the End of the matter.

The Marriage

The Ace of Swords, falling on the Desc., indicates disputes. Therefore, we may assume that they had been having considerable disagreement on how their joint affairs should be handled.

Throne VI indicates the most important factors. Card number 6 is Major Arcanum XVII, commonly read as *truth, hope or faith*. The fluid that flows from the two cups represents the forces of man and the forces of woman, and the blending of these forces indicates an exchange of finer energies which sustain each other. In one case the fluid is poured into the sea to indicate that nourishment of the emotions is necessary to gain inner truth. In the other case the fluid is poured upon the land to show the necessity of cultivating a positive, reasoning intellect to gain external truth. The eight-pointed star represents the balancing of male and female energies. So Major Arcanum XVII signifies that the newlyweds should recognize the importance of directing their energies properly. Card number 15 is reversed Major Arcanum VI, showing that *temptation* will present itself to lure them away from their objective.

Cards number 5 and 16, stationed on throne V, picture some of the modifying influences. Card number 5 is reversed Major Arcanum XX, commonly read as *awakening or resurrection*. Thus, if they attain the energy-exchange indicated by card number 6, this young couple will rise out of the old, negative influences leading to disputes, just as the figures symbolized on the card rise out of the coffin.

Card number 16 is reversed Major Arcanum II, indicating *science*. As two is always related to the sign Virgo, this indicates that analysis will fortify and sustain their awakening depicted by card number 5.

More details are revealed by the cards on Throne VII. Card number 7 is Major Arcanum XI, commonly read as *force, spiritual power,* or *fortitude.* This card advises the young couple to *accomplish their duties without hesitation* in order to defeat any actions prompted by temptation (card number 15 on Throne VI).

Card number 14 is reversed Major Arcanum XVI, which signifies *accident or catastrophe.* As it modifies the important factors revealed on Throne VI, the couple are warned to hold fast to their spiritual ideals (card number 7) or a marital catastrophe could result.

The Opposition

The Ace of Cups on the Asc. indicates that a *letter from a loved one* may present a certain amount of opposition to their marriage. Throne I gives the details. Here we find card number 1 to be reversed Major Arcanum XIX, pointing to *happiness or joy.* Card number 20 is the reversed Major Arcanum III, commonly read as *marriage or action.* As both of these cards are reversed, it appears that the letter will have a deep impact on either the husband or the wife who may experience a quickening of the emotions and be more susceptible to temptation.

Throne X holds cards number 10 and 11. Card number 10 is reversed Major Arcanum IX, which cautions that temptation should be met with *wisdom and prudence.* Card number 11 is Major Arcanum XVIII, and as it falls next to THE SAGE (XI), there is an indication that if wisdom is not employed, considerable *deception* could develop.

Cards on Throne II add detail to the important factors concerning the opposition. Card number 2 is reversed Major Arcanum XXII which shows that surrendering to temptation would be a great *mistake* possibly leading to the *failure* of their marriage. Card number 19 is reversed Major Arcanum IV, signifying that there is a *winning with will power*. The reversed position of the card denotes that it will take more effort than would be expected to withstand temptation.

The Progress

The Ace of Coins on the M.C. represents a *short journey*. On Throne VIII, card number 8 is Major Arcanum VII reversed, which points to *success through using intelligence*. Therefore, the mind should be kept open to insure a keen awareness while on the trip. Card number 13 is reversed Major Arcanum XII, which shows the possibility of a *sacrifice*. Card number 9, Major Arcanum I, portrays the *will and dexterity* required to apply intelligence when handling environmental influences. Card number 12 is THE WHEEL, or Major Arcanum X, presaging that regardless of how actions are influenced by a journey, changes are in store for the marriage.

The End

The Ace of Scepters on the M.C. can be read as *analysis in personal affairs*. Throne III holds card number 3, which is Major Arcanum XXI, pointing to *success and attainment*. Card number 18 is Major Arcanum XV, stressing the fact that *more is won through love than hate*. Although Major Arcanum XV is an adverse card, it is surrounded by beneficial cards. It would seem that if this young couple resolved the negative attitude depicted by this card, they would be able to maintain a harmonious partnership.

Throne IV holds cards number 4 and 17. Card number 4 is Major Arcanum V, read as *religion or law*. Card number 17 is Major Arcanum XIV, read as *regeneration*. If this young man and young woman learn to exchange finer energies to sustain a harmonious flow between them, they will be able to withstand the temptations that could bring trouble into their lives. If they remain faithful to each other and work together, their marriage will be strengthened and each will be regenerated.

4. THREE SEVENS SPREAD

This spread lends itself easily to short readings concerning questions embracing the past, present and future. Shuffle and cut the cards in the usual way and deal them according to the numerical sequence given in the diagram below.

The bottom row represents the Past, the middle row the Present, and the top row the Future. In each row the middle card is the Key Card and is the most important. The cards to either side of the Key Cards are subservient to the reading of the Key Cards themselves. In reading each row, the Key Card and adjoining cards modify each other and should be blended.

THREE SEVENS SPREAD DIAGRAM

21	20	19	18 KEY	17	16	15	FUTURE
14	13	12	11 KEY	10	9	8	PRESENT
7	6	5	4 KEY	3	2	1	PAST

Three Sevens Spread Demonstrated

A man who owned and operated a restaurant did not have enough capital to continue to run the business on his own. Consequently, it was necessary for him to find a partner. In the past, he had had a partner, but the association had not worked out. Although his former partner was pleasant and honest, the restaurant business was not his forte. Due to his past experience, the querent hesitated about taking on another partner to help finance the business.

These conditions motivated his question: "Will I succeed in a business partnership?"

When the cards were shuffled and dealt, they appeared in the following pattern.

9 SWORDS	9 COINS R	3 SWORDS R	XVIII R KEY	6 COINS	8 CUPS	2 CUPS
21	20	19	18	17	16	15

3 SCEPT.	2 COINS	10 COINS	VI KEY	H SCEPT. R	9 CUPS R	6 SWORDS
14	13	12	11	10	9	8

X	I SCEPT.	K COINS	K CUPS KEY	5 SCEPT.	XVII	4 CUPS
7	6	5	4	3	2	1

Reading

The names of the cards themselves are not mentioned in this reading. Rather, the cards are noted by the number of the sequence in which they fall. This number appears in parenthesis immediately preceding the key phrase. Furthermore, as the outcome of the question is known, the actual events of the past, present and future are interwoven into the reading.

Past

Due to the querent's financial difficulties, there had been a forced (1) *increase in the family.* Not only had he gained a partner, his partner's wife waited on table. (2) *Truth, hope and faith* describe the personality of the partner. His motives were good, and at first there was a (3) *success in the enterprise.*

The Key Card of the Past is the Cancer King, representing the old partner. He was (4) a *mild, reserved and homeloving man*. But the adjoining Gemini King indicates that there was (5) a *restless and fickle* side to his nature. This partner received (6) *news of a business opportunity,* which resulted in (7) a *change of fortune* for him. He returned to his former vocation —hairdressing.

Present

The querent needs to hold the thought of (8) *a slow, steady climb to success.* As the next card is reversed, (9) *the hopes will be realized* as a result of much effort. He is plagued by (10) *negative thoughts of business* as this card is reversed. Furthermore, he is advised to (11) *look beneath surface appearances.* This Key Card (11) represents the restaurant owner (querent) and depicts a man who can not decide which path to take. (12) *Alternate financial loss and gain* describe his present financial condition, which is quite unpredictable. (13) *Money acquired by hard labor* shows he must work hard to keep his business going, and this is exactly what he was doing when he asked the question. But because he couldn't keep up the hard pace and didn't have the needed cash, (14) *business partnership* was the solution. He was forced to take on a new partner.

Future

At first, the new partner considered the job as (15) *a work of love,* but soon he became (16) *extravagant* and then considered the job as (17) *a social event.* The Key Card, (18) *deception and false friends or secret foes,* signifies the new partner. His attitude upset the querent and caused strained relations. This led to a (19) *lawsuit or divorce.* And the partner's manner and the (20) *money he spent on associates* caused a (21) *quarrel resulting in enmity.*

At first the querent's partner viewed his job and the partnership as fun and a work of love. But then he began to overpay some of the employees to insure their loyalty. He proved to be a false friend of the querent when he took an outside job and still demanded his full half of the profits from the restaurant. When the querent refused to pay his half, his partner sued him and collected. After this incident, there was much tension at the restaurant until the partnership contract ran out.

MAGIC SEVEN SPREAD DIAGRAM

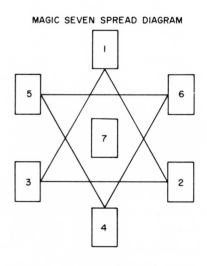

5. MAGIC SEVEN SPREAD

The points of this imaginary six-pointed star form 6 stations representing the past, present and future of the question asked. The seventh station in the center represents the result.

Shuffle, cut and deal the cards, following the numerical sequence on the diagram.

Significance of the Seven Cards

1. The past of the matter which caused the present condition.
2. The present, caused by the past as indicated by card 1.
3. The immediate future, which is brought about by combined past and present conditions.

4. This card shows the type of vibration that the querent must learn to handle in order to control the situation. It also represents those who favor a beneficial outcome of the matter and are able to help through their initiative and effort.
5. The effect of the surrounding environment on the matter.
6. Opposing forces.
7. Result of the question, brought about by the way the individual has reacted to the influences symbolized by the previous six cards.

Magic Seven Spread Demonstrated

A young man who had been successful as a dressmaker was trying to break into the more creative high-fashion field. To attract attention to his work, he designed a dress for a young lady to wear to a costume ball. His friends heaped praise upon his new creation. The gown attracted so much favorable attention at the ball that many felt sure it would win first prize. When it failed to win a prize, the designer was quite perplexed.

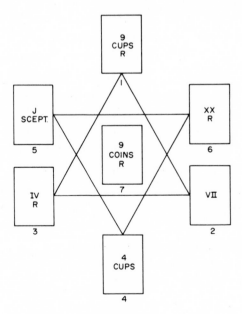

His concern prompted the question: "Why didn't my costume win a prize?"

When he consulted a tarot card reader, the cards were shuffled and cut, and then dealt into the pattern portrayed on the preceding page.

Reading

The first card dealt signifies the past of the matter inquired about and is the cause of the present condition. Here we find the reversed Nine of Cups, the *hopes will be realized*. This implies that the querent had had minor successes in designing gowns in the past. He was so emotionally (Cups) involved with his present creation and past successes that he had over-estimated his abilities.

The second card dealt represents the present and is the effect of past causes already indicated. Major Arcanum VII reads *perfection attained by active effort*. Because this is a *victory* card and is not reversed, it points to gaining success through hard work rather than relying upon emotion as indicated by card number 1.

The third card dealt denotes the past and present united and represents the immediate future of the matter. Card number 3 is Major Arcanum IV reversed, showing *confidence for proper development*. This seems to imply that the querent should place more faith in his work than in what people say about it.

The fourth card dealt indicates the power of the person to control the matter. It is also the influence of those favorable to it to control the matter through initiative and effort. Card number 4 is the Four of Cups. One of the readings for this card is *great joys are in store for you*. This card further implies, as it is co-ruled by Mars, that he should take aggressive action to fulfill his ultimate success.

The fifth card designates the part that environment plays

in the matter. Here we find the Jack (Youth) of Scepters, which indicates that a *young man of a Sagittarian disposition* or a Sagittarian environment could help the querent attain his goal.

The sixth card dealt shows environment and individuals in the future opposing the matter. Here we find Major Arcanum XX reversed, which reads *banish idleness with action.* Because the querent became easily depressed when he was not making speedy headway, this reversed card implies that the querent is his own worst enemy. This Major Arcanum XX also advises the designer to *broaden his mentality.* He should understand that creativity is nourished by wide and varied experiences.

The seventh card dealt represents the result of the thing asked about. The reversed Nine of Coins here reveals many things. The fact that it is a Coin card suggests money in the future—*money gained through inventiveness, sudden gain of fortune,* and/or an *unexpected gift from a friend.*

As soon as the reader finished the spread, he knew the querent had phrased his question improperly. What he actually had on his mind was: "Will I become a successful dress designer?" In other words, he was not interested in one costume ball, he was interested in a long-range view of his career. This situation clearly shows how important it is for the reader to know exactly what information is being sought. Unless the reader has this precise knowledge of the question, he cannot give a detailed reading.

The result of this spread was revealed a few months later. Soon after the reading was given, the young lady who had modeled his gown at the costume ball wore it to a party attended by many influential show people. As a result, the querent gained three new clients. These contacts inspired him to work harder, which the spread had implied he should do. Through an entertainer of a Sagittarian temperament, much attention was called to his work and opened the door to his ultimate success.

6. KABALA SPREAD

The Kabala Spread is used to determine the outcome of any question or situation. But more than this, it gives specific favorable and unfavorable influences leading up to the outcome.

The whole pack is shuffled and cut, then the top ten cards are laid out according to the sequence indicated by the diagram.

The three cards to the right in the diagram form the Tree of Good and indicate favorable forces and events.

The three cards to the left make up the Tree of Evil and point to unfavorable forces and events.

The four cards on the perpendicular line in the center, constitute the Tree of Life and represent the outcome.

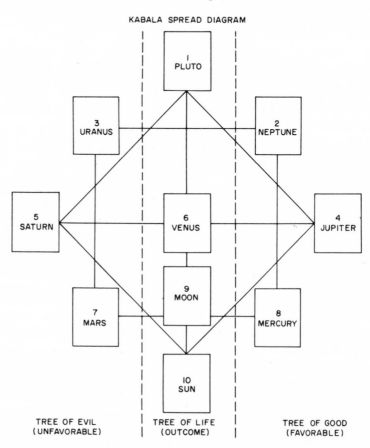

KABALA SPREAD DIAGRAM

TREE OF EVIL   TREE OF LIFE   TREE OF GOOD
(UNFAVORABLE)   (OUTCOME)   (FAVORABLE)

Significance of the Ten Cards

1.   (Pluto) Spiritual Result.
2.   (Neptune) Wisdom is the cause.
3.   (Uranus) Intelligence is behind it.
4.   (Jupiter) Mercy has an influence.
5.   (Saturn) Desire for Justice.
6.   (Venus) Love of Beauty, Love and Life.
7.   (Mars) Desire for Victory.
8.   (Mercury) Splendor and Show.
9.   (Moon) Home Conditions.
10. (Sun) Physical Power and Material Result.

Kabala Spread Demonstrated

When a man was asked to teach a class in astrology, he began to select his material and devise methods of presenting it.

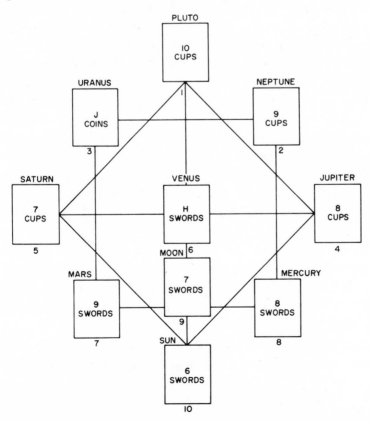

He knew that being the focal point of the class, the manner in which he conducted himself would result in its success or failure. So he asked the question: "How can I improve my platform personality?"

As he was already familiar with the tarot cards, he made the Kabala Spread himself. The ten cards for this spread fell as follows.

Reading

Card number 1, at the top of the Tree of Life, represents the Spiritual Result. It is the Ten of Cups, warning him to *avoid emotional crossfire* in order to allow his students to make the most progress in a harmonious atmosphere. If the constructive suggestions of this spread are adopted, the higher side of Pluto (Spiritual Result) will win out.

Card number 2, at the top of the Tree of Good, is the Nine of Cups. *Hopes will be realized* by an *analysis of thoughts, feelings, and actions.* As this is the station of Wisdom, the card implies that he does have the ability to attract success.

Card number 3, at the top of the Tree of Evil, is the Jack of Coins, indicating a *young man of an Aquarian temperament.* It is on the station of Intelligence. The intelligence in this case is not favorable to the class. What is indicated is that the querent will be faced with adverse, Aquarian-type responses from a young student. As the card is on the Tree of Evil, this student is interested in his own gain rather than in the progress of the group.

Card number 4, at the middle of the Tree of Good, is the Eight of Cups. The teacher's *uncontrolled sensitivity invites disaster,* if he tolerates extravagant and vague discussions. As the leader, he should demand the *blending of the practical with the ideal.*

Card number 5, at the middle of the Tree of Evil, is the Seven of Cups—*inspired by a psychic experience.* As this card is on the Tree of Evil, at the station of Justice, discordant entities may be attracted. He should check the inner plane source for authenticity before using any psychic ideas in class.

Card number 6, at the middle of the Tree of Life, is the Horseman of Swords, commonly read as *thoughts of enmity, strife, and sickness.* As this is the Venus station embracing Life and Love, he would find it more advantageous to think only harmonious thoughts about his class and to get proper rest and diet to prevent his becoming negative.

Card number 7, at the foot of the Tree of Evil, is the Nine of Swords. As this is the Mars station, he should beware of a *quarrel resulting in enmity.* If he would win Victory, he should control his temper. Antagonistic elements should be handled with charm and the light touch. He should *avoid the trap of propaganda* and check out the facts.

Card number 8, at the foot of the Tree of Good, is the Eight of Swords. This is the station of Splendor and Show. An enlightened, *enthusiastic approach severs limitations.* And if he practices his new-found self-control, he will prevent a *loss of prestige.*

Card number 9, on the Tree of Life, is the Seven of Swords, read as *ultimate gain through responsibilities.* As this card appears on the Moon station, it shows that the class could affect his Home Conditions. Because research and preparation of lecture material take time away from family activities, he should organize himself so that his home life will not suffer.

Card number 10, the bottom card on the Tree of Life, and the final card of the spread, is the Six of Swords. This may be read as *a firm stand avoids disorganization.* The negative aspect of the Sword Card can be handled by adopting a confident, Sun-like attitude.

It is interesting to note that the cards in this spread show four Cup cards and four Sword cards. Cups represent emotions and Swords depict struggles. From this we can say that controlling the emotions and planning action to cast out doubts and negative trends will lead to a favorable result.

The Kabala Spread, because of its Tree of Evil, deals with negative aspects. The card reader, therefore, has the moral responsibility to the querent to avoid the planting of negative seeds. The tarot reader should give him a true and thorough insight into the meaning of the cards so that he may better prepare himself to face any adverse condition.

7. SOLAR SPREAD

After shuffling and cutting in the usual manner, the cards are dealt from right to left in seven rows of seven cards each as illustrated in the diagram. Each card is turned over from top to bottom, and the cards are read as numbered.

Each row points to specific people, places and things ruled by the planet placed to the right of the row. The seven cards in the row show the Past, Present, and Future. The center card of the row represents the Present, the cards to the right depict the Past, and the three cards to the left of the center card denote the Future.

To more completely understand the nature of the planets and what they rule, the serious tarot reader should study the section on ASTROLOGICAL SYMBOLISM, PART IV. This will furnish more information which can be applied to reading the seven rows representing the different departments in life.

Significance of the Seven Rows

Moon—1st Row: home, domestic life, the public, women in general, and if the querent is a man, his wife.

Mercury—2nd Row: studies, travels, writing, papers, brothers and sisters, and intellectual activities.

Venus—3rd Row: love, affections, social activity, friends, partnerships, money and art.

Sun—4th Row: honor, superiors, health and vitality, men in general, and if the querent is a woman, her husband.

Mars—5th Row: creative energies, sex, strife, accidents, antagonisms and enemies.

Jupiter—6th Row: professional people, business, occupation, employment and religion.

Saturn—7th Row: elderly or serious people, real estate, sickness, losses, disappointments and secret things.

SOLAR SPREAD DIAGRAM

49	48	47	46	45	44	43	SATURN -- 7TH ROW
42	41	40	39	38	37	36	JUPITER -- 6TH ROW
35	34	33	32	31	30	29	MARS -- 5TH ROW
28	27	26	25	24	23	22	SUN -- 4TH ROW
21	20	19	18	17	16	15	VENUS -- 3RD ROW
14	13	12	11	10	9	8	MERCURY -- 2ND ROW
7	6	5	4	3	2	1	MOON -- 1ST ROW

FUTURE   PRESENT   PAST

Solar Spread Demonstrated

A worried divorcee with two children had not received any child support or alimony. She felt as if she had reached the end of her rope. In spite of her many talents, she had gone through a series of jobs. No job ever lasted long because she was so upset over her domestic problems. On top of this, her housekeeper robbed her and disappeared, never to be seen again.

The querent's upset condition and emotional problems resulted in excess weight and allergies which caused her skin to break out. When she felt she could go on no longer, she asked, "What does the future hold for me?"

The pattern which the cards took for her question was as follows.

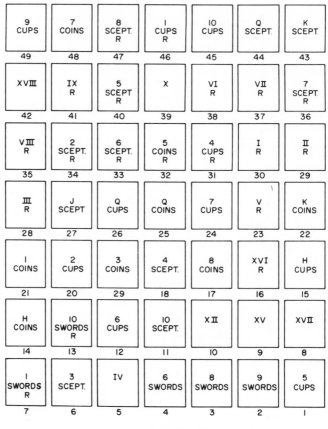

Reading

This reading is an excellent example of how the full knowledge of the querent's past conditioning can be helpful in reading a spread.

First Row

The seven cards appearing on the bottom row at the Moon station are related to the department of life embracing the home, domestic life and the public.

The first three cards on the right refer to the Past. Card number 1 is the Five of Cups, pointing to *a deep-seated attachment*. In the distant past the querent and her husband were deeply in love with each other, and when the children came, their love embraced them. They had a lovely spacious home with every comfort. The family was closely knit and did many things together.

The next card is the Nine of Swords, commonly read as *a quarrel resulting in enmity*. She and her husband went into business together. The business was successful, but as it expanded they became burdened with responsibilities. When the querent had to take on more than her share of work, she spent long hours at the office and was seldom home. Marital discord developed.

The third card is the Eight of Swords, signifying *dissipation through overwork*. In the business, she handled the office, and he made the public contacts. As time went on, they saw less and less of each other. It reached the point where they could not carry on a conversation without bristling. Eventually they obtained a divorce. She was given custody of their two children, and he was to pay child support.

This brings us up to the Present of the Moon Row represented by card number 4. It is the Six of Swords, denoting that *scattered energies bring sorrow*. At the time she asked the question, she had sold her large home and bought a smaller one, but was having a hard time meeting the payments. Another reading for this card is *trouble with your checking account*. Although she had been an efficient business woman in the past, the impact of her emotional upheaval left her mind more or less disorganized. Some of her checks bounced, and her utilities were turned off from time to time. But she continued to struggle (Swords) to keep the home together for the sake of her children.

Now we come to the Future of her Moon department, represented by the three cards to the left. Card numbed 5 is Major Arcanum IV which indicates *triumph over obstacles*. With a favorable card placed in this position of the immediate future, there is a promise of better conditions to come if proper actions are taken.

Because card number 6 is the Three of Scepters, she should

retain a dependable lawyer to review her affairs and help to focus her efforts. This card stands for *success in legal matters*. Futhermore, it is of the utmost importance for her to maintain a *jovial disposition* to furnish her children with a happy home environment. By keeping a harmonious frame of mind, better things relating to domestic affairs will be attracted.

The last card, representing the distant future, srikes a warning that action should be taken now to avoid trouble later. It is the reversed Ace of Swords and indicates *struggle to gain organization* that will result later, unless a solid plan is developed now and followed to the letter. Maintaining the jovial disposition noted in the last card will prevent *a depressed state of mind*.

Second Row

The seven cards in the second row from the bottom represent the Mercury department of life having to do with studies, travel, writing, papers, brethren and the fruits of intelligence.

The first three cards in this row (8-9-10) represent the Past. Card number 8, the distant past, is Major Arcanum XVII, commonly read as *truth, hope and faith*. When she and her husband started the business, they had faith that it would be a success. They were right. The fruits of their intelligence produced a flourishing business. But what she failed to recognize was that truth demands a blending of heart and mind.

Card number 9 is Major Arcanum XV which points to the fact that *greed brings eventual unhappiness*. She worked harder herself and drove her husband to make new contacts to bring in more business. Their efforts paid off, but she began to neglect her affectional life as she became more absorbed with office details.

Card number 10, Major Arcanum XII, shows *wasted effort*. Her driving ambition and concern with paper work was in a sense wasted effort. She and her husband separated at the peak of their business success. Her emotional let-down and dissappointment was so great that after this she could not even sit at her desk at home. Any typing, bookkeeping, or accounting (at which she had excelled) repulsed her. When she attempted any of these mercurial pursuits, she would actually become physically ill.

With three Major Arcana (cards 8-9-10) appearing in the Past, these activities importantly affected her present condition.

Card number 11 represents the Present of the Mercury department of her life. Here we find the Ten of Scepters, signifying *an invention or discovery*. At the time she asked the question, her personal papers, bills, legal briefs and so forth were in a confused hodge-podge. To go forward it would be necessary for her to overcome her repulsion of Mercurial duties. Ten is the number denoting change. It would be imperative for her to adopt *new business methods*.

Cards 12, 13, and 14 are concerned with the Future Mercury department of life. The immediate future is described by card number 12 which is the Six of Cups. Six always refers to temptation, therefore, she should *check her hunches* and *carefully analyze her emotions* before making any decisions involving paper work.

The next card is the reversed Ten of Swords indicating a *sudden loss of employment,* which could come about if she continued to view desk work with distaste. Unless she changed her attitude, she could become *her own worst enemy.* This is especially true since her experience was along the lines of accounting, auditing and bookkeeping. It was absolutely necessary for her to keep a job, for unless she worked, she could not maintain her home and children.

Card number 14 is the Horseman of Coins, representing *thoughts of health and money.* As the previous card (13) was concerned with sudden loss of employment, this card (14) ties in with it. It is especially significant as it emphasizes thoughts of a negative nature in association with her attitude concerning mercurial associations.

Third Row

The seven cards in the third row from the bottom indicate the Venus department of life associated with love, society, friends, partners, cash and art.

The first card of this row (15) is the Horseman of Cups and well describes the *thoughts of love and affection* which bound the family into a warm embrace and attracted many kind friends. These contacts paid off handsomely in the first months of their business.

Card number 16 is reversed Major Arcanum XVI. This is the Mars or *catastrophe* card. When the querent became completely absorbed in the business, she spent less time with her friends. *You reap what you sow.* Later when she approached her friends for moral and financial help, they let her down—she had broken the contact.

The next card (17) is the Eight of Coins, commonly read as *a costly law suit.* At the time she and her husband split up, their personal affairs were completely entangled with the successful business, which had to be disposed of. Her husband was obligated to pay some of the creditors. When he failed to do so, she was sued. It cost her plenty in legal fees to prove her inability to pay. In the meantime, her husband had filed bankruptcy papers. Futhermore, he had not paid any child support. *Marital litigations* also proved costly for her.

Now we come to the middle card which represents the Present. Here we find the Four of Scepters—*honor gained through initiative.* She had moved to another area and had no friends there. As she could not afford to join a club or organization, she threw herself into charity work for a few hours a week. Here, her organizational ability (for someone else) gained her much praise. Through it, she was invited to join a bridge club, one of her pet hobbies. In her adjustment from the old to the new life, this activity served as a stop gap. She yearned to be surrounded by well-known, successful people, as she had been in the past. She felt strongly that her early success came when she was *influenced by people in authority.*

Cards number 19, 20, and 21 represent the Future of this department of her life. The 19th card is the Three of Coins foreshadowing *gain through social activity.* In this area of her life, this card suggests that she direct her vocational talents into social spheres rather than plod behind the scenes.

Card number 20 is the Two of Cups pointing to *emotions guided by reason.* If her vocation takes her into the social swim, she will have the opportunity to cultivate a wider circle of friends—the kind she had in her happier days. But to maintain these friendships, her *emotions must be guided by reason.*

Card number 21 is the Ace of Coins which means *social contacts for financial gain.* This card refers to the distant future. If she is selective in cultivating her contacts, especially among intellectual and scientific people (Ace), hers will be a *social contact for financial gain.*

Fourth Row

Four rows up from the bottom are the seven cards relating to the Sun department of life which covers honor, health and vitality, and men.

Card number 22, the first card of the Past, is the King of Coins, a *person of a Gemini temperament.* This card well describes her husband. In addition, it marks the atmosphere they lived in when they were first married. In true Gemini fashion they had lots of fun and a sense of humor which allowed them to hurdle obstacles with ease. They are both mental types. They had much in common and were expert bridge players. Spilling with vitality, they were loved by all.

Card number 23 is reversed Major Arcanum V. When they pooled their talents in the business world, they received *favors from professionals,* which quickened their climb to success as they built up solid credit. But her reputation began to suffer when trouble developed between them.

Card number 24 is the Seven of Cups indicating *resolution of domestic discord,* which came about with their divorce. Later she learned that while she had been so involved with the business, her husband had become enamored with another woman.

Card number 25 (Key Card) represents the Present of this department of her life. Here we find the Queen of Coins, depicting her current *Libra temperament.* Libra desires to balance things, but she had come to a point which loomed like the eleventh hour. She was indecisive (Libra), and asked, "What do I do next?"

Card number 26 represents the immediate future. As the Queen of Cups appears here, in the near future, a *woman of a Scorpio nature* may enter her life.

Card number 27 is the Jack of Scepters. The woman of a Scorpio nature, shown by the previous card, will perhaps introduce her to a *young man of a Sagittarian nature* for business (Scepters) reasons.

Card number 28, the last card of this row, is reversed Major Arcanum III. The new contacts mentioned above could provide her with *success in creative pursuits.* However, as card number 28 is reversed, she should keep these relationships on a business level. Even though business success can come through *social activity,* she is cautioned against following the *line of least resistance.*

Fifth Row

The Mars Row embraces the department of life having to do with accidents, antagonisms, and enemies.

Card number 29 is reversed Major Arcanum II, picturing the splendid *intellectual exchange* between her and her husband. At first this exchange was so sparkling and harmonious that they knew no animosity.

Card number 30 is reversed Major Arcanum I, indicating *changeable influences.* Her absorption in the business and her long work hours caused fatigue, and her judgment was affected.

This resulted in careless actions which attracted accidents. She crushed her fingers when shutting the car door, and she slipped on the wet kitchen floor and broke her ankle.

Card number 31 is the reversed Four of Cups, signifying an *exposé of a revengeful plot*. Her husband was not only unfaithful to her, after their divorce he tied up the business with bankruptcy proceedings. He was her secret enemy until one of her lawyers exposed him.

Card number 32 (the Present) is reversed Five of Coins, which may be read as *help through neighbors*. The querent confided her problems to a neighbor who tried to help her by doing this spread. If the querent took the advice of the reader, this could have been a *profitable contact*. However, as the card is reversed, the querent may not have taken full advantage of the reading.

Card number 33 is the reversed Six of Scepters. Six is always the number of temptation. Therefore, the querent was advised to *seek moderation* and *avoid extreme measures in business*. She would be able to side-step antagonism if she *emphasized moderate aims and goals*.

Card number 34 is the Two of Scepters. Because this card is reversed, she would need to take extra effort to gain the *esteem of her co-workers*. If she *watched her interests with vigilance,* she would attract less enmity and antagonism.

Card number 35, reversed Major Arcanum VIII, may be read as *worry attracts discordant events*. With the Mars department (fifth row) so discordant in this reading, the querent was told that *every action brings a reaction*. Worry and brooding are negative states, which when coupled with over-aggressiveness, lead to accident. She should practice *moderation in all things*.

Because all of the cards in this row are reversed, the Mars area in her life should be carefully watched and properly handled so that she will attract a more harmonious future.

Sixth Row

The Jupiter Row contains the seven cards which deal with

the department of life affecting business, occupation, employment and religion.

Card number 36 is reversed Seven of Scepters. In the past she was extremely efficient about business. She could *rely on her own judgment* to make proper decisions.

Card number 37 is reversed Major Arcanum VII, read as *victory,* denoting that she had the *power to command others.* It was she who hired, counseled and fired the employees in the business. However, as the reversed positions of this and the previous card indicate, her run-down condition from overwork and emotional problems robbed her of these special talents.

Card number 38 is reversed Major Arcanum VI. With her divorce topping her troubles, she found it difficult to *stabilize her emotions.* When she went out on her own, she attracted a succession of good jobs. But her biggest fault was telling her troubles to everyone, including the boss. As a result, each job she had was short-lived. This lack of security kept her in a constant state of worry about paying her bills.

Card number 39 (the Present) is Major Arcanum X, which shows the wheel of fortune turning. At the time she asked the question, she was unemployed. She was undecided whether she should look into a new line of work or return to an office job. She had a strong urge for a *change of fortune* in her vocation and wanted to *break the old tie* with her former type of work. It should be remembered that THE WHEEL, which represents radical changes (Uranus), can turn in either direction.

Card number 40 is reversed Five of Scepters, her immediate Future in the Jupiter department. As five is keyed to Jupiter, it denotes that she should remain in the professional world. However, the reversed card position indicates a strong need to *practice faith* in order to demonstrate a new position which would suit her.

Card number 41, reversed Major Arcanum IX, indicates that more *wisdom and prudence* should be used in planning her activities. When a position is offered, she should not be *blinded by outward appearances* but should take *a cautious psychological approach* to learn the requirements and advantages of the job.

Card number 42 is Major Arcanum XVIII. The approach described by the previous card would allow her to *place herself in a better environment*. Then, once established, she should remember that *too much sympathy emphasizes discord* and attracts *deception*.

Because the sixth row contains five Major Arcana, she should be deeply concerned with the factors associated with this department of life.

Seventh Row

The top row of the spread embraces the Saturn department of life which is concerned with elderly people, real estate, sickness, losses, sorrows and secret things.

Card number 43 is the King of Scepters. When she decided to sell her large home and buy a smaller one, she contacted an *Aries type* realtor. He talked her out of selling her adjoining property separately from the house. Later, to her disappointment, she learned that she could have sold this property separately to greater financial advantage.

Card number 44 is the Queen of Scepters. After selling her large home and property, she tried to dispose of her lake-side cabin. To initiate this transaction, her husband's signature was necessary. Several lawyers tried for months to get it and failed. Finally a lawyer (a *woman of a Leo temperament*) obtained his signature.

Card number 45 is the Ten of Cups. Ten always refers to change. When she found a buyer for the large home, he wanted to take possession immediately. This *sudden change in the home* caused the querent to become emotionally distressed. Even though the house had been up for sale for some time, she had not really given it up in her heart. She was forced to quickly *reverse her feelings*.

Card number 46 is the Ace of Cups, representing the Present. She accustomed herself to the new, smaller home, but was hard put keeping up the payments. At the time the reading was made, she had *traveled concerning domestic affairs,* which made it possible for her to have a tarot reading by the former neighbor. While there, the querent was trying to negotiate a loan on some property she still held in the town she had moved away from.

Card number 47 is reversed Eight of Scepters, which shows that *business success through initiative* is her key for the immediate Future. Number eight stands for crystallization, and the reversed position of this card indicates that she must exert more effort to gain business success.

Card number 48 is the Seven of Coins. Through *directed mental energy* she will be able to *solve the problem* and have *a profitable business trip.*

The distant future of the Saturn department of life is shown by the wish card—the Nine of Cups, indicating her *hopes will be realized.* As it is reversed, she should *analyze her thoughts, feelings, and actions* before consummating any business deal.

8. WISH SPREAD

The Wish Spread is used when the querent wants to know if something definite will come to pass.

First, the reader selects a card to represent the querent and places it face up in the center. For example, if the querent is a Virgo man, the reversed Queen of Swords may be used to represent him. However, it is possible to use any card in the entire pack, selecting one which most closely corresponds to the querent's appearance or mood at the time the question is asked. For example, a question having to do with a love affair may be represented by the Six of Cups, commonly read as *a love affair.*

After selecting the card to represent the querent, the reader fans the remainder of the deck face down on the table. Then the querent draws fifteen cards at random holding his question strongly in mind. (The remaining cards are re-collected and set aside as they are not used.)

Now, the querent shuffles and cuts the fifteen selected cards in the common manner, and the reader deals them face down, one at a time, as shown in the diagram on page 78.

Significance of the Card Groups

1- 2- 3   What surrounds you.
4- 5- 6   Factors describing your wish.
7- 8- 9   What opposes you.
10-11-12   What comes to your home.
13-14-15   What you will realize.

Significance of the Wish Card

The Nine of Cups is always called the wish card. If it appears anywhere in this spread, except on 7, 8, or 9, the wish, at least in part, will be realized. How soon the wish will be realized is determined by the placement of the wish card. The closer it appears in numerical sequence to card number 1, the sooner the wish will be realized. But if the wish card falls on 7, 8, or 9, in all probability the wish will not materialize, and these three cards will show why.

If the wish card fails to appear in the spread, it does not necessarily mean that the wish will not come true. To determine if the wish will come true, the tarot reader examines the cards to see whether they are mostly favorable or unfavorable.

Wish Spread Demonstrated

After one of her successful parties, a lady discovered that her gold watch was missing. The last time she remembered seeing it was when she set it on the sideboard near the kitchen sink. As her friends had a habit of bringing uninvited guests with them, she was in a quandary about who might have taken it. Her strong motivation for having a reading was, "I wish I had my watch back."

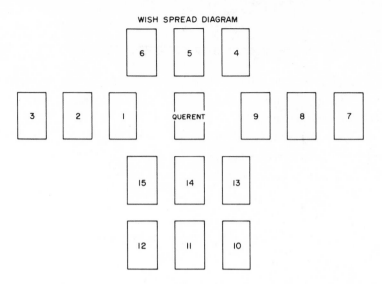

As the querent was intelligent, restless and fickle, the King of Coins in a reversed position was selected to represent her. This card was then placed in the center.

The tarot reader fanned the cards on the table, and the querent selected fifteen of them at random. After the remaining cards were set aside, the fifteen cards were shuffled and cut by the querent. They appear below as dealt by the reader.

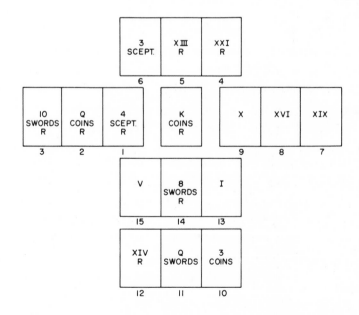

Reading

(This spread illustrates the effectiveness of applying the information contained in PART IV, ASTROLOGICAL SYM-BOLISM. Things, represented by the planets or signs to which the cards are keyed, may be chosen in place of or in conjunction with given phrases according to the subject matter.)

What Surrounds You

Card number 1 is the Four of Scepters, commonly read as *a legacy,* but because the card is reversed, it could point to a loss. Since Leo is ruled by the Sun which rules gold, we may assume that the card represents the gold watch. Furthermore, the Leo decanate of Leo could describe the party which the querent gave.

Card number 2 is the reversed Queen of Coins, indicating a *Libra type man:* tall and well formed, clear complexion, sparkling eyes, hair brown or black.

Card number 3 is the reversed Ten of Swords, showing that this man, due to a *sudden loss of employment,* may have entertained the idea of pawning the watch.

Factors Describing Your Wish

Card number 4 is Major Arcanum XXI, bearing the symbol of the Sun. As the card is reversed, it again indicates her concern and her hopes of recovering her gold watch *through perseverance.*

Card number 5 is Major Arcanum XIII which is reversed and keyed to the sign Aries. This shows further mental agitation. The common key phrase is *transformation* and suggests the end of an old condition and the beginning of a new one.

Card number 6 is the Three of Scepters, directing her to employ *aggressive action* in order to take constructive advantage of the change shown by card number 5.

What Opposes You

Card number 7 is Major Arcanum XIX, indicating *happi-*

ness or joy. Card number 8 is Major Arcanum XVI, representing *accident or catastrophe.* And card number 9 is Major Arcanum X, which depicts a *change of fortune.* These cards seem to indicate that the Libra man, who was assumed to have taken the watch, at first enjoyed the financial security derived from the sale of the watch. However, there is an indication that some sort of accident (8) may have caused him to change (9) his mind about his past actions.

What Comes to Your Home

Card number 10 is the Three of Coins. The number three indicates action, and because Mercury appears on the card, action may be taken through conversation, a phone call or a letter.

As card number 11 is the Queen of Swords, the conversation, phone call, or letter could originate with a *woman of a Virgo temperament.*

Card number 12, reversed Major Arcanum XIV, following the Queen of Swords, points to subject matter which could revolve around personal property or money, as indicated by the sign Taurus.

What You Will Realize

Card number 13 is Major Arcanum I, showing that physical obstacles (cube symbol in lower right-hand corner of card) may be overcome by *will power* and proper mental (Mercury) activity.

Card number 14 is the reversed Eight of Swords, an unfavorable card ruled by Saturn, indicating a loss yet showing an opportunity to gain in character growth through this *experience.*

As card number 15 is Major Arcanum V, the whole experience will have a strong impact upon her philosophy of life, as indicated by Jupiter.

In surveying these three cards, one might jump to the conclusion that the watch would be recovered. Such a reading might spring from the fact that the last card in the spread is the favorable Major Arcanum V, ruled by the benefic planet Jupiter.

However, there are certain factors to be considered before drawing a final conclusion. The wish card does not appear in the spread. Seven of the fifteen cards are reversed. And the majority of the cards are unfavorable.

9. SPREAD OF 36

The whole pack is shuffled and cut three times in the routine manner, and thirty-six cards are dealt face down as illustrated in the diagram. The remainder of the cards are set aside.

Significance of the Rows

Cards	1- 6	Past
Cards	7-12	Present
Cards	13-36	Future

First, the cards of the Past, Present and Future are read in their numerical order. Then, because past actions always influence the present and future, more information concerning the question can be gained by pairing cards number 1 and 36, 2 and 35, 3 and 34, ending with cards 18 and 19.

SPREAD OF 36 DIAGRAM

36	35	34	33	32	31
30	29	28	27	26	25
24	23	22	21	20	19
18	17	16	15	14	13
12	11	10	9	8	7
6	5	4	3	2	1

Spread of 36 Demonstrated

A talented young lady, whose artistic drive had forced her into many projects, felt she was getting nowhere. She asked, "What can I do to get more accomplished for the time I put into my work?"

Her question led to a spread showing the cards grouped as in the diagram on page 85.

Reading

According to the directions given, the Past, Present and Future, as well as Supplementary Information based upon card pairs, are read as below.

Past

Card number 1 is the reversed Queen of Scepters. *A Leo man* was responsible for placing her in motion pictures early in life.

Card number 2 is Major Arcanum XX indicating an *awakening.* By associating with creative people, she found that *through perception there is awareness.* As a result of these theatrical associations, other avenues of creativity were opened to her.

Card number 3 is Major Arcanum XI. When she tried to expand her activities, she met obstacles. Fortunately, through her study of metaphysics, she learned to *advance with faith.* Then she realized that *obstacles are more imaginary than real.*

Card number 4 is the Eight of Swords. In her enthusiasm she took on numerous artistic activities, and the *added responsibility* brought worry.

Card number 5 is the Five of Cups, indicating *a deep-seated attachment,* which she claimed absorbed too much of her creative energies. This experience taught her to *hold her emotions in check.*

Card number 6 is Major Arcanum XIX, which shows that

self organization attracts contentment. In other words, this sums up her past motivation which led to her question.

Present

Card number 7 is the reversed Four of Cups, which may be read as *a strong and lasting friendship.* Card number 8 is the reversed Four of Scepters indicating a *successful enterprise.* Card number 9 is the reversed Queen of Swords showing a *man of a Virgo temperament,* who acted in the manner indicated by card number 10, the Eight of Coins—*support from a friend.* Card number 11 is Major Arcanum XXI which stands for *attainment,* and card number 12 indicates the *victory* of Major Arcanum VII.

The Virgo man had become her lasting friend, and he was able to open so many doors for her that she found herself occupied with many creative endeavors. She had attained success in decorating for his social gatherings, designing television scenery, and trimming the windows of smart dress shops. On top of this, she was writing a book about the famous people she had met and worked for.

Future

Card number 13 is reversed Major Arcanum II, which indicates that one of the best things she can do in order to produce more in a shorter length of time is to *keep her intentions silent.* Too much talking about her projects will not only dissipate her energies, it will consume time which could be spent in the materialization of her ideas.

Card number 14 is the Youth of Coins, which shows either a *young man of an Aquarian temperament* or an Aquarian environment.

Card number 15 is the reversed Major Arcanum VIII, which could be read as *all work, no play makes Jack a dull boy.* This then, implies that card number 14 is to be read as an Aquarian youth rather than environment. He could be so mentally stimulating that she might find it easy to come up with original ideas. *Pleasure stimulates more productivity.*

Card number 16 is Major Arcanum VI, commonly read as *temptation*. This card verifies her past history. When she gets too involved in romantic interests, her creative output suffers. In view of this, her association with the Aquarian youth should be handled with care. She should *stabilize her emotions* to keep the relationship on a mental level, so that she will be able to *resist sensualism*.

Card number 17 is the reversed Three of Coins, which indicates *profit from partnerships*. As this card sometimes points to *success in selling*, it could symbolize an opportunity, which, if she grasps it, will allow her to marshal and direct her creative talents.

Card number 18 is the Five of Coins, which further emphasizes *money through original ideas* or *reward from writing*. This card, and the previous card, foreshadows the possible acceptance of the book that she has in preparation.

Card number 19 is the Two of Scepters, which signifies a *healthy frame of mind*, which could come as a result of her *success in a business venture*.

Card number 20 is Major Arcanum III, which points to *social activity*. With her many influential contacts, this could portray her appearance at autograph sessions, television interviews, and parties in her honor.

Card number 21 is the Horseman of Swords, indicating *thoughts of enmity*. When a person in the querent's position realizes success, there are sometimes those who would not give her credit due to jealousy. At such times, it would be well for her to recognize this trait and guard her reactions accordingly.

Card number 22 is reversed Ten of Scepters, which can be read as a *variety of personal activities*. With her time consumed by the above-mentioned social activities, there is no doubt that little time would be left for her to be creative. The number ten always stands for change.

Card number 23 is the Four of Swords, which is commonly read as *remorse for past action*. She will finally come to realize that she has unbalanced the scales.

Card number 24 is the reversed Horseman of Coins, denoting *thoughts of money*. It is one thing to have a good time, but when we socialize too much the billfold becomes thin. This card infers that in order to reach her goal of accomplishing more in as little time as possible, she must balance social life with her work life.

Card number 25 is the Five of Swords, which indicates that she will *benefit by re-organizing her working environment*. If she does this, she will dissipate the feelings of remorse (pictured by card number 23) and experience the *lifting of a restriction*.

Card number 26, which is the Horseman of Scepters, shows that her *thoughts* may then turn to *business*.

Card number 27 is the Two of Cups. The number two always stands for science. Therefore, this could well describe her *love of research* which could direct her into a new business project.

XV	2 SWORDS	3 CUPS	I SWORDS	9 SCEPT.	XII
36	35	34	33	32	31
6 CUPS	J CUPS	Q CUPS R	2 CUPS	H SCEPT.	5 SWORDS
30	29	28	27	26	25
H COINS R	4 SWORDS	10 SCEPT. R	H SWORDS	III	2 SCEPT.
24	23	22	21	20	19
5 COINS	3 COINS R	VI	VIII R	J COINS	II R
18	17	16	15	14	13
VII	XXI	8 COINS	Q SWORDS R	4 SCEPT. R	4 CUPS R
12	11	10	9	8	7
XIX	5 CUPS	8 SWORDS	XI	XX	Q SCEPT R
6	5	4	3	2	1

Cards number 28 and 29 indicate men who will probably be involved in the same project. The reversed Queen of Cups represents a *man of a Scorpio temperament,* and the Youth of Cups represents a *young man of a Pisces temperament.*

Card number 30 is the Six of Cups. As this and the previous three cards are Cup cards, an emotional environment is indicated. Six always stands for temptation. So we may assume that here again she is faced with a situation where she should use *constructive activity to overcome sensualism.*

Card number 31 is Major Arcanum XII, which signifies she can be triumphant, as it reads *material temptation conquered.*

Card number 32 is the Nine of Scepters. Following on the heels of the last five cards, it would appear that by conquering her temptation she could have *a wise and profitable friendship* with the men involved in the new business referred to under card number 27.

Card number 33 is the Ace of Swords, indicating a period marked by *delays in intellectual pursuits,* as well as *difficulty in adjustment.*

Card number 34, which is the Three of Cups, points to the fact that in spite of delays, her *ideals can be realized through positive action.*

Card number 35, however, is the Two of Swords, emphasizing *struggle* (Swords). As two is associated with Virgo, her progress will depend upon analysis. She should realize that she can gain mental *development through struggle.*

Card number 36 is Major Arcanum XV. Even though this is a discordant card, it is a signboard re-emphasizing for her that *delays can be avoided by careful planning.* Furthermore, the *deceptive and distintegrated activity* associated with this card can be avoided by *overcoming pride and self-interest.*

Supplementary Information

Now we come to the part of the spread where we start picking the cards up in pairs—cards 1 and 36 being the first pair. As key phrases for two cards are not listed in Part III, the following pair readings are the results of combining the basic influences of the two cards involved in each pairing. To demonstrate, we will now read the eighteen pairs of cards.

1 and 36: Too much social activity could be her downfall.

2 and 35: A practical, scientific approach leads to an awakening.

3 and 34: Cultivating the proper creative mood would allow her more artistic and dramatic expression.

4 and 33: The top rung of the ladder can be achieved through hard work and a strong will.

5 and 32: Love and loyalty to friends brings business rewards.

6 and 31: True happiness often demands certain sacrifices.

7 and 30: To gain realization, temptations must be overcome.

8 and 29: Business rewards realized by associating with a Pisces youth.

9 and 28: Be prepared to cope with quick tongues and sharp minds.

10 and 27: Warns again of the necessity for balancing the head and the heart.

11 and 26: Proper thoughts attract success in business.

12 and 25: Take legal precautions in matters of publication.

13 and 24: Unless the two sides of a situation are properly weighed, a loss of money or health could result.

14 and 23: A young man of an Aquarian temperament could inspire her to work with determination in expressing her artistic talents.

15 and 22: A change of business methods to establish equilibrium.

16 and 21: A strong defense against physical temptation is a constant, loving companion.

17 and 20: Creative action leads to financial rewards.

18 and 19: Properly applied inspiration results in financial and mental compensation.

10. MAGIC CROSS SPREAD

After shuffling and cutting the deck three times, the cards are dealt in the form of a cross. Deal five cards in a horizontal line from left to right. Then deal eight more cards in a vertical line, crossing the horizontal row at right angles as illustrated in the diagram.

Significance of the Thirteen Cards

1 and 2—the past.
3—the present.
4 and 5—the opposition.
6 and 7—hopes and expectations.
8 through 13—the future.

MAGIC CROSS SPREAD DIAGRAM

Magic Cross Spread Demonstrated

Enthused with the study of occult science, a talented young man wanted to know what his cosmic mission was. He said he would rather be an adept in occult philosophy than a clergyman. From the philosophical and spiritual literature he had read, he realized that spirituality is synonymous with unselfishness. He asked, "What can I do to contribute more to humanity?"

Following is the Magic Cross spread for his question.

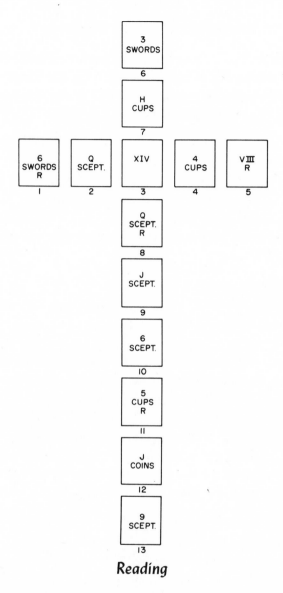

Reading

(Although this reading is religious in topic matter, the Magic Cross spread may be used for any type of question.)

The Past

The card on the extreme left arm of the cross is the reversed Six of Swords, commonly read as *dissipation*. Relating to the past, it plainly indicates that as a result of this young man's turning away from the common, material life, his thoughts gave him a glimpse of the inner life.

The next card to it also relates to the past and is the Queen of Scepters, signifying that a *woman of a Virgo temperament* had a great influence upon the decision that he made.

The Present

The card common to both cross arm and upright is Major Arcanum XIV; it relates to the present. And as the popular meaning of this card is *regeneration,* it shows his desire to transmute his energies into their highest expression for the good of humanity.

The Opposition

Any opposition to the actions he might take is represented by the two cards to the right of the upright. The first of these is the Four of Cups, implying the tendency to *over emphasize his emotions.* To quell this opposition, he should be moderate in his thoughts, feelings and actions. That is, he should avoid both extreme enthusiasm and abject depression.

Furthermore, as the next card to the right is reversed Major Arcanum VIII, to control opposing forces he should concern himself with seeking *moderation in all things.* This card warns him against becoming over enthusiastic, as his buoyant mood could be deflated by the least obstacle or provocation.

Hopes and Expectations

The two top cards on the upright above the cross arm picture his hopes and expectations. The top one of these is the Three of Swords, which could be read as a *divorce* from old conditions. This card not only denotes his desire to become more spiritual, but shows the necessity for him to release old ideas in order to utilize his energies in unselfish acts.

The next card down from the top is the Horseman of Cups, commonly read as *thoughts of love and affection.* As this is a Scorpio card, there is a great deal of intensity motivating his desire to love humanity as a means of developing into a spiritual master, or adept.

The Future

The six cards below the cross arm represent successive conditions or events in the future and give a clue to the actions he should take to reach his goal.

Picturing the immediate future is the reversed Queen of Scepters, referring to a *man of a Leo temperament*—the querent. The Leo emphasis gives him a clue as to the manner in which he should face the future to accomplish his goal.

He would profit by meditating upon the best and worst qualities of Leo. (See ASTROLOGICAL SYMBOLISM, PART IV.) He should cultivate a humble, kindly attitude about the responsibilities he will attract if he is to accomplish his mission. Willfulness, domination, or getting a swelled head about his progress will prevent him from attracting opportunities to serve and thus develop.

The next card down is the Youth of Scepters, indicating that his area of activity could well be among *young men in the business world.* It further shows the necessity for him to become an outstanding example of an upright character, expressing sound religious (Sagittarius) principles.

As the next card down is the Six of Scepters, *music, art or drama* will have a strong appeal to him. Since six is the number of temptation, before putting his time into such activities, he should consider how to tie their influences into furthering his chosen goal.

Then comes the Five of Cups, which is commonly read as *good fortune in love.* As it is reversed, he will have to take extra effort at times, due to environmental *responsibilities,* to maintain a feeling of universal love, not allowing personal love to affect any judgment (Jupiter) he might be called upon to make.

The following card is the Youth of Coins, indicating a *man of an Aquarian temperament.* This card also points to the querent, showing certain traits he should encourage, such as the friendly, psychological and intellectual approach; and the traits he should discourage, such as argumentativeness, extremism, and eccentricity. (See ASTROLOGICAL SYMBOLISM, Aquarius.)

The last card is the Nine of Scepters, commonly read as a *wise and profitable friendship.* This could indicate that once he has developed the habit systems which coincide with spirituality, a counselor from the inner planes will impress him with facts that will assist him in his mission.

As five of the cards in the spread are people cards, this young man's work is with groups, especially young men in business. By developing the talents signified by the cards, he could do considerable missionary work. In addition to becoming an example of the spiritual life himself, he will be able to grasp ever-present opportunities to plant seeds in young minds, encouraging others to espouse the spiritual way of life themselves.

If spiritual desires and motives are kept high, his mind can be reached by inner-plane members of the legions of light and be impressed to take such stands and actions that will assist him in his work of making this a better world in which to live.

II. LIFE SPREAD

This spread may be used effectively to give a general life reading regarding the material, intellectual, and spiritual trends. After shuffling and cutting the cards, they are dealt face down in the sequence shown in the diagram. When each card is turned over from top to bottom, it is read as a subsequent event or influence in the life.

Material Square

Cards number 1 through 28 form the Material Square. These cards represent activity on the physical plane. As physical and mental activities are closely interwoven, only physical events and conditions, having no direct bearing on intellectual pursuits or spiritual attainment, are considered. Therefore, these cards stand for such things as the physical body, public attainment, money and people.

Mental Trine

Cards number 29 through 40 form the Mental Trine. These cards indicate activity on the mental plane. They correspond to concentration, intellectual attainment, studies, opportunities for acquiring knowledge, and suggestions for the development of directed thinking.

Spiritual Circle

Cards number 41 through 49 form the Spiritual Circle. These cards symbolize activity on the spiritual plane. They relate to the moral trend and opportunities for spiritual growth and point to character traits to be developed to attain a spiritual goal.

Dominating Life Factor

Card number 50, in the center of the diagram, bears special significance. The most important events occurring on each plane throughout the entire life have been read in the square, the trine and the circle. Card number 50 indicates, on all three planes, the dominant influence in shaping the life of the querent.

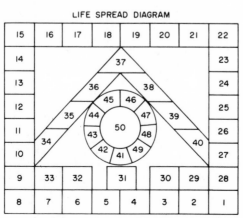

LIFE SPREAD DIAGRAM

Life Spread Demonstrated

A woman asked for a general life reading. When the cards were shuffled and dealt, the depicted layout below resulted.

Reading

Because this reading is so long, the card number appears in parentheses before each key phrase.

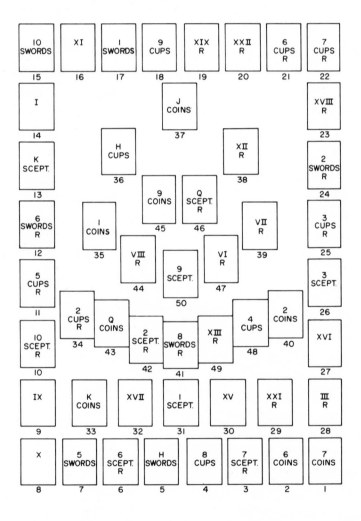

Material Square

While living in the eastern states, the querent had found that (1) *money could be earned through a journey,* pictured by the Seven of Coins. She had discovered that her type of work paid a higher salary on the west coast, so she moved there. She obtained a higher paying position in assembly line work and also (2) *gained by original ideas,* depicted by the Six of Coins.

While working there, she discovered that (3) *personal philosophy wins popularity.* She soon learned that there were certain flaws in her personal philosophy and personality which some of her co-workers disliked. These flaws are indicated by the reversed position of the Seven of Scepters. Card number 4, which is the Eight of Cups, tells her that she must (4) *blend the practical with the ideal* in order to be more readily accepted by her co-workers.

The attitude of her co-workers is prompted by her own (5) *thoughts of enmity,* depicted by the Horseman of Swords. As the next card, Six of Scepters, is reversed, she is warned that if she does not learn to win the respect of her co-workers, she will not progress in her job. She should realize that (6) *promotion comes through the ability to rule others* with a constructive approach.

The Five of Swords shows the (7) *end of a legal battle* as well as (7) *quarrels about possessions.* The divorce from her first husband resulted in strife over the division of property. Therefore, we may assume that these cards highlight conditions which have occurred in her life up to this point. This fact is emphasized by card number 8, Major Arcanum X, which is commonly read as a (8) *change of fortune.* The next card is Major Arcanum IX, suggesting that if (9) *wisdom and prudence* are exercised in the future, her life will be more successful.

The Ten of Scepters reversed may be read as (10) *victim of eccentric afflictions.* Therefore, she should (11) *hold her emo-*

tions in check, as indicated by the reversed Five of Cups. She should learn from past experiences that her discordant emotions attracted an unfortunate marriage as well as strife with co-workers.

Card number 12 is the Six of Swords reversed. The feeling that this card implies is (12) *struggle can lead to progress.* Because of its reversed position, we can reasonably assume that the struggle will be difficult. At the same time, however, she should realize that this struggle, as depicted in this material square, is simply a link in the chain leading to mental and spiritual progress and should be thought of as an interesting challenge.

The King of Scepters may indicate a (13) *man of an Aries temperament* or may depict a more fiery and ambitious state of mind adopted by the querent. Fortunately, the following card, Major Arcanum I, shows that through her (14) *will or dexterity* she can (14) *win over obstacles.*

The Ten of Swords, placed in the upper left-hand corner of the square, suggests that (15) *she could be her own worst enemy,* but (16) *advance with faith* is denoted by Major Arcanum XI.

So far the querent seems to have had alternate gains and losses. However, many of the cards appear to indicate that she could advance more rapidly in the physical world by developing stronger mental and spiritual qualities.

The Ace of Swords shows not only (17) *faulty analysis,* and (17) *division of ideas,* but also the (17) *inability to talk fluently.* Possibly these traits were formed due to her (18) *search for domestic harmony* after the loss of her first husband coupled with a (18) *strong desire for affection.* The symbolism on the Nine of Cups card advises that (18) *analysis of thoughts, feelings and actions* may overcome some of the problems which card number 17 implied.

If she takes this advice and learns to (19) *align her physical, mental and spiritual goals,* she will find (19) *happiness and joy* as denoted by Major Arcanum XIX. Because the card is reversed, she must exert some effort in order to reap the benefits symbolized by this card.

Reversed Major Arcanum XXII further implies that (20) *indiscretion could be her downfall.* The reversed Six of Cups emphasizes again that she should (21) *carefully analyze her emotions.*

Reversed Seven of Cups indicates that she could be (22) *inspired by a psychic experience.* But since the card is reversed, as in the following Major Arcanum XVIII, she should beware right from the start that (23) *abuse of occult powers invites destruction.* The Two of Swords reversed shows a (24) *difficult road to success.* However, the Three of Cups reversed indicates that effort will lead to (25) *ideals realized through positive action.*

Activities relating to her physical world seem to come from (26) *action in church affairs,* symbolized by the Three of Scepters. Because of the various readings of the cards so far in this spread, we can assume that the querent has a tendency to dissipate her energies. This tendency is one of the discordant qualities of Mars, the planetary key to (27) Major Arcanum XVI. She should, therefore, (27) *save her energy for constructive pursuits.*

The sooner she realizes that (28) *thoughts are things,* as indicated by Major Arcanum III, she will be well along the proper road leading to material success. However, because it is reversed, if she takes the (28) *line of least resistance,* she could stumble on the rocky road of (28) *unbalanced activity.*

Mental Trine

Cards number 29 through 40 embrace the grand trine of mental activity. Card number 29 shows Major Arcanum XXI reversed (THE ADEPT), commonly read as (29) *success and attainment.* Again, perhaps, her reward may come through hard work, as this card appears in a reversed position. THE BLACK MAGICIAN (Major Arcanum XV) follows, warning that (30) *material ambition should be balanced with mental pursuits.* In other words, because of the past implications of this spread, the querent is the type of person who could be so carried away in her quest for mental knowledge that she could be a burden to herself, friends and loved ones in forgetting her material obligations.

But (31) *honor may be gained from mental activity,* as shown by the Ace of Scepters. Because we have already concluded that there will be some struggle in her mental advancement, she should be reminded that (32) *overcoming problems strengthens character,* as implied by Major Arcanum XVII.

Card number 33, the King of Coins, represents a Gemini influence. Because it is upright, we may surmise that its influence is harmonious rather than discordant. A thirst for knowledge (Mercury) seems to be represented here instead of a (33) *man of a Gemini temperament.*

Following is the Two of Cups reversed, signifying a (34) *love of research.* This could possibly indicate much reading as it follows the Gemini King and precedes the Ace of Coins, which may be read as (35) *love of study.* Because these cards are followed by the Horseman of Cups, harmonious (36) *thoughts of love and affection* are coupled with this research and study. Therefore, a beneficial outcome should be expected from these pursuits.

Then it appears that a (37) *male youth of an Aquarian temperament* (Jack of Coins) will have some influence on her mental activity.

Major Arcanum XII reversed reads as the (38) *material world may dominate the soul.* This seems to tell us that the previous card (37) does represent a youth, and that this youth may, after a time, have to be sacrificed to insure her further mental development. It should be remembered that through (38) *disappointments* a person is strengthened by learning lessons from experiences. Such character development leads to (39) *victory,* shown by reversed Major Arcanum VII and (40) *rewards through mental effort,* shown by the Two of Coins, the last card in the mental trine.

Spiritual Circle

The Eight of Swords reversed commences the spiritual circle and shows a (41) *struggle to maintain balance.* The reversed Two of Scepters signifies that (42) *obstacles can be resolved through analysis.* The following Queen of Coins could denote a high-minded (43) *person of a Libra temperament* or that a Libra frame of mind could well aid the querent in her spiritual growth. She must, however, (44) *develop a spirit of give and take* as indicated by reversed Major Arcanum VIII.

The Nine of Coins tells us that (45) *mental possessions endure longer than physical.* If she develops a (46) *strong will,* symbolized by Leo on the reversed Queen of Scepters, she will be able to overcome (47) *temptation* as depicted by reversed Major Arcanum VI, and advance her spiritual attainment. If she follows the advice given by the last three cards in this spiritual circle, she will find that (48) *great joys are in store for her,* as pictured by the Four of Cups.

Major Arcanum XIII reversed, is commonly read as (49) *tranformation.* By developing her material, mental, and spiritual attributes, she will be blessed beyond her widest imagination, for (49) *immortality is promised.*

Dominating Life Factor

The overall influence in her life, on all three planes of endeavor, is depicted by card number 50, which is the Nine of Scepters.

The number nine stands for wisdom and prudence. And Scepters stands for business. As the querent is not married, the business world will furnish the most suitable channels for the expression of her energies in a manner which will contribute most to humanity.

From ditch-diggers to great spiritual leaders, all have a part to play in the wheel of life. Each individual should strive to find his special type of work and activity. As far as the querent is concerned, her key is seen in the Sagittarius-Leo decanate of card number 50. By applying the kindness and confidence of

Leo and the faith and enthusiasm of Sagittarius, she will develop on all three planes by facing and overcoming the problems she meets in the business (Scepters) world.

12. FOUR TRINES HOROSCOPE SPREAD

While the cards are not put down in the order of horoscope houses, the reading of each card does reveal what may be expected relative to the particular department of life ruled astrologically by the horoscope house in which the card is found. The cards are shuffled and cut three times, and then they are dealt in the diagram sequence.

Significance of the Four Trines

Trine of Life
    Card 1 personal life: health
    Card 6 mental life: philosophy, publishing, travel
    Card 11 life of posterity: children, love affairs, pleasures, speculation
Trine of Power
    Card 2 power to attract honor and authority: business, credit, reputation
    Card 7 power of environment: sickness, inferiors, labor
    Card 12 power of wealth: cash, personal possessions
Social Trine
    Card 3 society of partners: husband or wife, known enemies, lawsuits
    Card 8 society of kin and thoughts: brothers and sisters, studies, writing, short trips
    Card 9 society of associates: friends and well-wishers
Trine of Concealed Things
    Card 4 concealed things in environment: the home, real estate, the end of life
    Card 10 concealed things related to others, money: legacies, debts, taxes
    Card 5 concealed afflictions: disappointments, restrictions, unknown enemies

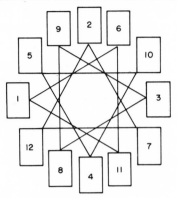

Four Trines Horoscope Spread Demonstrated

When a young married man with children asked about the immediate future of all areas in his life, the following horoscope spread resulted.

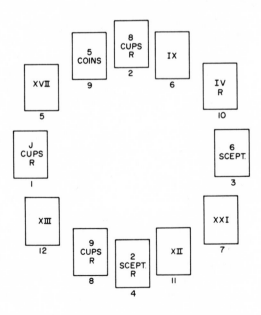

Reading

Although key phrases may be used for this spread, we chose not to employ them in order to delve more deeply into the symbology of the cards. Furthermore, the readings are brief, but they form the springboards from which the experienced tarot reader may provide more detailed explanations.

Trine of Life

Card number 1 is the reversed Jack of Cups, indicating an emotional trend which could upset his personality and ultimately affect his health. Uncontrolled emotions might lead to a weight problem, as the sign Pisces, pictured on this card, is conducive to weight.

Card number 6 shows THE SAGE. The querent was deeply interested in occult studies. But recently he had so many responsibilities that he was not able to pursue these studies. The Aquarian rulership of this card signifies a contact with a friend which could well lead to the broadening of the querent's outlook. Since this card is upright and harmonious and falls on the station of philosophy, it presages a mental life which could bring rich rewards.

Card number 11 is THE MARTYR. As the querent enjoys little recreational pleasure, due to working seven nights a week to support his wife and children, this card seems to imply that he may soon be called upon to make a greater sacrifice for the sake of his children. Or possibly another child could bless his household. In any event, added responsibility is shown.

Trine of Power

Card number 2 is the reversed Eight of Cups, showing some discord in this particular department of life. For the sake of his family, in the past he had to make a personal sacrifice. He is a musician who plays in a restaurant where he feels that his talents are not fully appreciated, although the job pays well. As the card is reversed, it shows no release from his frustration in the near future.

Card number 7 is THE ADEPT. In the near future, he could experience harmonious relations with co-workers on the job. The previous difficulties indicated by cards 1 and 2 are modified by the influence of this Sun card, which points to a strong vitality.

Card number 12 is THE REAPER. In the near future he will probably be faced with strong opposition regarding his income. This period will be one of transition which will give him cause for thought about supporting his family.

Social Trine

Card number 3 is the Six of Scepters. This station, closely associated with the public, shows that music—one of the arts depicted by this card—will affect his future and be tied in with a benefic influence. As this station also represents his wife, the card points to continued happiness with an understanding and loving wife.

Card number 8 is the Nine of Cups reversed. Recently, he returned to college during the day, while continuing to work nights. Because the wish card falls here, apparently he will accomplish what he has set out to do. Being reversed, the card warns him to organize and apply himself in order to complete his schooling.

Card number 9 is the Five of Coins, indicating that he may make profitable contacts with friends and neighbors who will be in a position to help him reach his goals.

Trine of Concealed Things

Card number 4 is the reversed Two of Scepters. In the near future he may have the opportunity to teach music pupils at home to supplement his income. However, such a venture could affect his home environment, not only for him but for his wife and three children as well.

Card number 10 is THE SOVEREIGN reversed. In this context, the card reveals a possibility that he will have difficulty in meeting the monthly bills. But because it is a card of regeneration, after a struggle he will probably make it.

Card number 5 is THE STAR. This is the last card in the spread. The blazing star of truth, hope, and faith signifies that his deep philosophical attitude, which he seldom reveals to others, will carry him on to surmount the obstacles pictured in his future.

13. TWELVE HOROSCOPE HOUSES SPREAD

After shuffling and cutting the cards, they are dealt in the numerical sequence shown in the previous Four Trines Horoscope Spread Diagram.

However, they are read in horoscope fashion, starting with card number 1 representing the first house and reading counterclockwise to end with card number 5, representing the twelfth house.

Significance of the Twelve Horoscope Houses

1st House:	the physical body, personality, disposition, and personal interests.
2nd House:	money and personal possessions.
3rd House:	brothers and sisters, private thoughts and studies, neighbors, short trips.
4th House:	the home and its environment, the father.
5th House:	pleasures, love affairs, speculation, children and entertainment.
6th House:	working environment and co-workers, illness, tenants and pets.
7th House:	marriage, partnerships, the public, known enemies, competitors, and law suits.
8th House:	death, debts, taxes, gifts and legacies, insurance and mortgages, and other people's money.
9th House:	teaching, publishing, advertising, lecturing, long trips, religion and philosophy, and the court.
10th House:	honor, business, reputation, profession, superiors and the mother.
11th House:	friends, hopes, and wishes.

12th House: self-undoing, disappointments, restrictions, unknown enemies, institutions and charitable influences.

Twelve Horoscope Houses Spread Demonstrated

A recently widowed woman was left with a 12-year-old son. And even though she inherited a small home, her husband had not carried life insurance. She had not worked during her marriage, but after her husband passed on, she managed to secure a clerical job which paid little.

Concerned over the welfare of her son and her own future, she asked the question, "What will I have to do to improve all areas in my life?" The cards fell as shown below.

Reading

The first house of the chart (card 1) is occupied by the reversed Five of Swords. The suit of Swords points to struggle and affliction. This seems to indicate that she will *gain through*

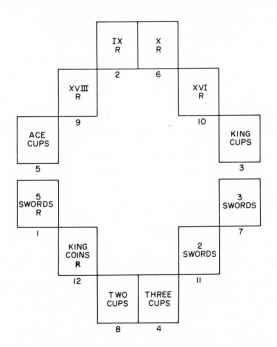

hard work. Whatever comes to her personally (first house) will not come easily (Swords).

The second house of money (card 12) shows the reversed King of Coins, indicating that a *woman of a Gemini temperament* may be responsible for influencing her financial prospects. (Refer to Gemini in PART IV, ASTROLOGICAL SYMBOLISM, for additional material to expand this subject matter.)

The Two of Cups (card 8) is found in the third house. As Two refers to science and Cups to emotions, a healthy, well-balanced state of mind is indicated—*passion controlled by reason.* She should maintain this attitude as it will help her in some of her less fortunate houses.

The fourth house, governing the home and its environment, holds a fortunate card—the Three of Cups (card 4). This indicates that she should hold on to her inherited home for the benefit of her son and herself. She should have *faith in her actions.*

The fifth house (card 11) ruling her 12-year-old son, holds the Two of Swords, which is commonly read as *sickness through overwork.* In the absence of a father, her son might feel a sense of responsibility and a lack of security. This could lead him to overwork in order to protect his mother. The mother should not let her concern about money affect the boy, as this might cause him to develop a financial complex which he could easily carry into his adult life.

The Three of Swords (card 7) is located in the sixth house, ruling her working environment. This card indicates that she may feel *held down by responsibility.* Therefore, it would be well for her to use *organized activity to overcome adversity.* Because the sixth house also rules health and is associated with the suit of Swords, she should take positive action (three) to maintain a healthy condition so that she can continue to care for herself and her son.

The King of Cups (card 3), appearing in the seventh house, could portray a *man of a Cancer temperament* entering her life, either as a marriage or business partner. It may also indicate a kindly attitude toward her from the public. With this fortunate card placed on this angle, she would probably meet little opposition from the public.

THE LIGHTNING, Major Arcanum XVI (card 10), is in a reversed position in her eighth house. As this card is keyed to the planet Mars, she could attract strife and discord in associating with the lending or borrowing of money. In addition, even at work, she would be ill advised to handle other people's money.

The ninth house, ruling religion and philosophy, holds reversed Major Arcanum X (card 6). THE WHEEL in this department of life shows that her *change of fortune* will undoubtedly lead to the adoption of new philosophical concepts. *New conditions replace the old.*

The tenth house (card 2) holds reversed Major Arcanum IX, showing that in order to protect her reputation as a widow with a child, all of her actions should be tempered with *wisdom and prudence.* Also, because this is an Aquarian card, she should be on the alert to adapt to any job (tenth house) changes.

The eleventh house (card 9) of friends shows the reversed Major Arcanum XVIII, commonly read as *deception, false friends, and secret foes.* This indicates that friends frequently fail to live up to her expectations and that she should *choose her companions carefully.*

The twelfth house (card 5) holds the Ace of Cups, indicating *a sympathetic mental turn.* However, she should remember that self-undoing (twelfth house) comes from being over sympathetic, *a mood demanding analysis.*

14. INDIVIDUAL HOROSCOPE SPREAD

The tarot puts the flesh on the bones of astrology, as it supplies the esoteric significance which astrology alone lacks. Therefore, this method enables you to understand the deeper significance of your own life, stressing in particular the mental and spiritual elements. It is an effective means of pin-pointing the aids and helps associated with the various natal horoscope factors which will, if applied, assist in character growth—the highest function of either astrology or the tarot.

This method of reading your horoscope is not divinatory in nature as are the other spreads in this section, for scientific principles are employed as a frame of reference.

The specific data required for casting your horoscope is the exact longitude and latitude, the date, and the hour, of your birth. Once this information is acquired and the horoscope is correctly calculated, you will be able to apply this valuable spread to your own personal advantage.

As the key vibrations in the individual horoscope have already been established, the period of concentration, shuffling, cutting and dealing become unnecessary.

Whether you merely visualize or actually place the cards in the pattern of your natal horoscope, the added knowledge gained by reading these positions will help to uncover the nature and motivations of your innermost thought urges. If it is inexpedient for you to actually place the cards in the form of the horoscope, you may visualize their appropriate positions.

As only the twenty-two Major Arcana are used, they should be removed from the deck. To read your chart completely, the twelve zodiacal cards corresponding to your birth-chart house cusps should be placed around the wheel. Next, place the ten planetary cards in the house positions corresponding to the planets in your birth chart.

After forming this pattern, you will be able to note what might be expected from the houses where the cards fall. This is done by judging the combinations shown by the cards, when united, according to the astrological aspects in your horoscope.

This method may be carried further and applied effectively to progressions. Progressed aspects depict energy in one or more departments of life, and because of the various planets and houses involved, they often form complex groupings which are difficult to delineate. At these times you may require additional information when conflicting testimony leaves you in doubt. This situation may arise in any branch of astrology—natal, mundane, horary, or weather predicting. Combining the cards according to the aspects and conditions of any chart often brings factors to light which will make the answer clear.

One progressed aspect alone may hold uncertain implications. For instance, take the seventh house. It rules both marriage partnership and business partnership. For explanatory purposes, let us say that a man and wife are in business partnership when a discordant progression forms. Does this indicate a threat to the marriage partnership, to the business partnership, or to both?

The discordant progressed aspect could map all three conditions. To determine which condition is indicated, the YES OR NO SPREAD may be utilized to define its meaning. One of the following specific questions could be asked: "Does this progressed aspect mean the end of my business partnership?" or "Could this aspect mean the breakup of my marriage?"

After these questions are answered, another spread may be selected to answer the question, "What can I do to prevent the discord shown by this progressed aspect?" Then when the advice is applied, there is an opportunity to transmute the discordant energy of the progression into constructive channels and thus divert tragedy.

The foregoing demonstrates how astrology and the tarot—the two keys opening the gates to nature's sanctuary—can be used to better the life.

Part III

KEY PHRASES FOR THE 78 TAROT CARDS

*B*efore we study each individual card, a quicker grasp of the subject may be gained by taking a panoramic view of the whole pack. This approach will enable us to tuck into our minds the associated astrological symbolism. Then the subconscious will be furnished with a wealth of material to draw upon when we start to study each individual card.

A complete tarot deck consists of:

22 Major Arcana	40 Minor Arcana
16 Court Arcana	78 Cards

Major Arcana: these 22 cards are associated with the 10 planets and the 12 signs of the zodiac. *Minor Arcana:* these 40 cards are associated with the 36 decanates and the 4 quadrants of the zodiac. *Court Arcana:* these 16 cards are associated with the 12 signs and the 4 quadrants, or fixed signs (Jod-He-Vau-He), of the zodiac.

Major Arcana

Here are listed the 22 Major Arcana accompanied by their numbers, astrological associations, and card names:

I	Mercury	THE MAGUS
II	Virgo	VEILED ISIS
III	Libra	ISIS UNVEILED
IV	Scorpio	THE SOVEREIGN
V	Jupiter	THE HIEROPHANT
VI	Venus	THE TWO PATHS
VII	Sagittarius	THE CONQUEROR
VIII	Capricorn	THE BALANCE
IX	Aquarius	THE SAGE
X	Uranus	THE WHEEL
XI	Neptune	THE ENCHANTRESS
XII	Pisces	THE MARTYR
XIII	Aries	THE REAPER
XIV	Taurus	THE ALCHEMIST
XV	Saturn	THE BLACK MAGICIAN
XVI	Mars	THE LIGHTNING
XVII	Gemini	THE STAR
XVIII	Cancer	THE MOON
XIX	Leo	THE SUN
XX	Moon	THE SARCOPHAGUS
XXI	Sun	THE ADEPT
XXII	Pluto	THE MATERIALIST

Minor Arcana

The 40 Minor Arcana consist of 10 numbers expressing 4 different elements—fire, earth, air and water. Each card, according to its number, corresponds to some astrological subdivision of the 22 Major Arcana. The four elements mark the suits, which signify the departments of life: Business, Love, Money and Struggles.

Scepters indicate the fire signs: enthusiasm, ambition and enterprise. Their reading is directed to Business, Occupation,

Station and Honor. Scepters represent the fire of Summer.

Cups indicate the water signs: sympathetic, receptive and submissive. Their reading is directed to Emotions, especially Domestic and Affectional Relations. Cups represent the festivities of Autumn.

Swords indicate the earth signs: patient, industrious and practical. Their reading is directed to Struggle and Affliction. Swords represent the hardships of Winter.

Coins indicate the air signs: changeable, sociable and mentally alert. Their reading is directed to Health or Money. Coins represent the balmy air of Spring.

Each Minor Arcanum corresponds to a ten-degree section of the zodiac, called a decanate. This decanate is designated by the two sign symbols which appear in the upper right-hand corner of the card. The first symbol represents the actual sign of the zodiac, while the second symbol stands for its decanate.

The nine Minor Arcana of each suit correspond to the nine decanates of each zodiacal triplicity, and the tenth card embraces the whole triplicity, symbolizing a transition to a new cycle.

Aries, Cancer, Libra and Capricorn, the movable, pioneer signs, form the true point of departure in any triplicity when establishing tarot correspondences. Thus, the first fire sign of a movable nature is Aries; the first movable water sign is Cancer; the first movable air sign is Libra; and the first movable earth sign is Capricorn.

Note that the departure for establishing tarot correspondences is not determined by zodiacal sequence, but by movable signs. For example, even though Taurus is the first earth sign of the zodiac, it is ruled out because it is not a movable sign, but a fixed sign. Capricorn, even though it comes near the end of the zodiacal sequence, must be the point of departure of the earth triplicity, because it is the only earth sign of a movable nature.

SUITS	SCEPTERS	CUPS	COINS	SWORDS
ACES	♈ - ♈	♋ - ♋	♎ - ♎	♑ - ♑
TWOS	♈ - ♌	♋ - ♏	♎ - ♒	♑ - ♉
THREES	♈ - ♐	♋ - ♓	♎ - ♊	♑ - ♍
FOURS	♌ - ♌	♏ - ♏	♒ - ♒	♉ - ♉
FIVES	♌ - ♐	♏ - ♓	♒ - ♊	♉ - ♍
SIXES	♌ - ♈	♏ - ♋	♒ - ♎	♉ - ♑
SEVENS	♐ - ♐	♓ - ♓	♊ - ♊	♍ - ♍
EIGHTS	♐ - ♈	♓ - ♋	♊ - ♎	♍ - ♑
NINES	♐ - ♌	♓ - ♏	♊ - ♒	♍ - ♉
TENS	FIRE LION ♌ JOD	WATER EAGLE ♏ HE	AIR MAN ♒ HE	EARTH BULL ♉ VAU

The list above graphically presents the astrological correspondences of the 40 Minor Arcana. For interpretation of these symbols, see PART IV, ASTROLOGICAL SYMBOLISM.

Court Arcana

There are 16 Court Arcana. To represent different types of people, 12 cards (Kings, Queens and Youths) are assigned to the temperaments as depicted by the twelve signs of the zodiac. The remaining 4 Court cards (Horsemen) indicate the kind of thoughts these different types of people think. The Kings, Queens and Youths (sometimes called Jacks) describe the 12 basic temperaments of people; and the Horsemen indicate the thoughts they think.

The following arrangement was chosen to maintain the sequence of the zodiacal signs for easier association. Hence, the suit headings do not appear in the same sequence as those in the table above.

This panoramic view of the tarot deck shows us that the 78 cards are based upon the 10 planets, the 12 signs with

SUITS	SCEPTERS	SWORDS	COINS	CUPS
KINGS	♈	♉	♊	♋
QUEENS	♌	♍	♎	♏
YOUTHS	♐	♑	♒	♓
HORSEMEN	FIRE LION ♌ JOD	EARTH BULL ♉ VAU	AIR MAN ♒ HE	WATER EAGLE ♏ HE

their 36 decanate divisions, and the 4 quadrants of the zodiac. Therefore, it is easy to see that a knowledge of astrology is a necessity to an expert tarot reader. Nevertheless, the cards may still be used without the knowledge of astrology, but depth of meaning will certainly not be as complete without recourse to the basic astrological symbolism.

Phrase Selection

Grasping the basic principles and developing the ability to apply them marks the competent card reader. A reader who relies on "lists" of card meanings alone does not clearly understand the synthesis of the fundamentals. If he merely consults a list, he will continually be faced with "conflicts" between one card and another.

Lists are valuable for the beginning student as an aid to the study of the fundamentals. But in the last analysis interpretation is based upon symbolic principles, not lists, which have merely sprung from the principles.

Taking the symbolic principles behind the Nine of Cups will demonstrate this. The number 9 stands for wisdom and prudence (indicated by Major Arcanum IX). It is associated with the sign Aquarius. The suit of Cups points to emotions, especially domestic and affectional. The card is also keyed to the water-sign Pisces as well as to its third decanate, sub-ruled by Scorpio. Both Pisces and Scorpio are double rulership signs (two planets ruling one sign); therefore, Neptune, Jupiter, Pluto and Mars are involved. On the card, only one of the rulers—Pluto—of the Scorpio decanate is pictured. However, a reader with a knowledge of astrology will bring in the other planets involved.

By way of illustration, here are two key phrases listed under the Nine of Cups.

1. *Passion supplanted by exalted love.* The key phrase in its entirety implies emotion, which is depicted by the suit of

Cups. *Passion* is symbolized by Scorpio or Pluto. *Supplanted* indicates the application of wisdom and prudence (9) to an emotional problem. *By exalted love* springs from the astrological symbolism of Neptune, which is the higher octave of Venus (love).

2. *Strong desire for affection.* *Strong desire* is shown by the intense sign Scorpio, and *affection* is associated with the suit of Cups.

To learn how to fashion key phrases from the basic symbolism on your cards, a splendid exercise in training is to take each phrase listed under each card in this section and tie the words in with the symbolism represented by the card. Then soon you will be speedily forming your own original phrases keyed to that specific symbolism.

Aside from astrological symbols, the 22 Major Arcana contain drawings keyed to other symbolism. The symbolism of these pictures appearing on the Major Arcana has been so completely covered in the book "The Sacred Tarot", by C. C. Zain, it is not repeated here. The space it would take to do this has been used more advantageously to clarify card reading.

There is no end to what can be gained by meditating on any card. Let's look at Major Arcanum I, for instance. The two outstanding symbols to catch the eye are the Roman numeral I at the top of the card and the capital A at the bottom of the card. Does it not seem logical that our pack of 78 tarot cards should start with the number I and the letter A—both long used by man to represent a beginning of something?

In the upper right-hand corner we see the symbol Mercury, the messenger of the gods. Since time immemorial, Mercury has been synonymous with mind. Even before the formation of the universe, it must have first been conceived in the mind of the Creator. And still today before anything manifests physically it is first conceived within a mind (Mercury). How often have we heard that we must watch the thoughts that we think for "thoughts are things"?

Since the number I and the letter A imply a beginning, we may assume that some form of action is implied. Mercury also points to activity which should be guided by reason. For any activity to result in success, will power is needed. The man pictured on Major Arcanum I stands tall and firm, symbolizing the attitude of will which precedes action.

The double gesture made by his hands is significant in its symbolic meaning. The right hand points to heaven representing his constant search for mental enlightenment, and the left hand points to earth denoting his desire to conquer physical obstacles with the knowledge gained. It also shows a strong will to dominate all acts of life by the spirit.

In the lower right-hand corner of the drawing we find a cube or square representing physical obstacles which must be overcome to learn life's lessons.

The sacred ibis of Egypt on the side of the cube indicates that physical limitations (represented by the cube) are surmounted only by constant vigilance.

On top of this cube lies a sword, a coin, a cup and a cross, the latter being used to symbolize the Scepter on the tarot cards. This quartet, representing the four tarot suits, symbolizes lessons to be learned through struggle, money, emotions, and business.

The white robe worn by the man signifies purity of body and mind, original or regained. His belt is portrayed by a serpent biting its tail, which always symbolizes eternity. The gold circlet around his head stands for enlightenment and universal expression.

Manipulating Symbols

The symbolic drawings on each of the Major Arcana may be interpreted in the above manner. However, in the case of the Minor Arcana and the Court Arcana, we rely more upon astrological symbolism than pictorial symbolism. Emphasis is placed upon the astrological signs, decanates, and planets, in addition to the tarot suits.

For example, look at the 16 Court Arcana. All of them are face cards. The 4 Kings, 4 Queens, 4 Youths (Jacks) are associated with twelve signs of the zodiac: Kings to the first four signs; Queens to the second four signs; and Youths to the last four signs.

The zodiacal signs are of four elements—fire, earth, air and water—to which the tarot card suits relate: fire to Scepters, earth to Swords, air to Coins, and water to Cups.

The 4 Horseman cards correspond to the four quadrants of the zodiac. Each one is identified with one of the fixed signs: Leo-fire-Scepters; Taurus-earth-Swords; Aquarius-air-Coins; and Scorpio-water-Cups.

The common interpretation of the Kings, Queens and Youths is a person of a certain nature. For instance, the King of Scepters indicates a *man of an Aries temperament*. However, if the King of Scepters is reversed, the card indicates a *woman of an Aries temperament*.

In either case, it should be understood that the indicated person does not have to be born under the sign of Aries. All the card tells us is that the person has Aries traits. This again demonstrates that the more one knows about astrology, the deeper he will be able to delve into tarot symbolism.

Rather than representing a person, a Court card is often read as a modifying environmental influence, the nature of which is described by the astrological symbolism on the card. Examples of this can be found in the Pyramid Spread Demonstrated in PART II of this book.

However, when the Court card stands for a person, his influence on the querent's life is portrayed by the card immediately preceding it. And the action this person will take or the moves he will make are shown by the card that next follows in the spread.

The Horsemen cards stand for thoughts or unseen intelligences influencing the life of the querent. The person who thinks the indicated thoughts is represented by the Major Arcanum nearest the Horseman in the spread. To signify the carrying power and astrological significance of thought, the horsemen are mounted. Favorable thoughts and plans are indicated when they fall right end up. In reversed position, they show thoughts or unseen intelligences detrimental to the interests of the querent.

To glean a wider meaning and scope to your key phrases for the Court cards, turn to PART IV, ASTROLOGICAL SYMBOLISM. There will be found a wide variety of items keyed to the sign shown on the Court card under consideration. One may be selected which ties in with the question content, helping the reader to gain a more complete estimate of the forces at work.

In reading any tarot card, your own results will depend upon the magic or alchemy of your own personal thinking and imagination. With practice, you will find your mind using the Law of Association, linking pertinent symbols together into meaningful and telling concepts. Sometimes using two or more key phrases for the same card will result in a more descriptive interpretation. This is done effectively in the Solar Spread Demonstrated in PART II.

After you study this book, you will see that reading the tarot cards is not child's play. The fundamentals are simple, but because they may be applied to any and all facets of the universe, the ramifications are unlimited. Even though the choices of key phrases for each card are several, the basic beat or key tone is the same. Experience leads to right choices, which, when reached, bring not only a helpful reading but a glow of self-satisfaction.

Universal Symbolism

Common human experience is what universal symbolism is

based upon. Regardless of where people live or what tongue they converse in, the language of universal symbolism is understood. Through the centuries human nature has not changed much, and man's reactions remain basically the same. Therefore, first responses to a symbol by the ancient Chaldeans probably was no different from, say, members of the United Nations today.

For instance, a cloud suggests rain; and lightning, thunder. Then, in addition to the natural symbols, early peoples drew pictographs to record their interests and warnings. Finally, as man evolved, symbols and allegories, revealing important thoughts to be conveyed to others, were passed down through generations.

History piled up a record of associations which form this language of universal symbolism. The more familiar you become with these widely known symbols, the easier you will be able to interpret your tarot cards. Explanations of common symbolism may be found throughout this book, and specific associations for each sign and planet are classified in **PART IV, ASTROLOGICAL SYMBOLISM.**

The application of universal symbolism allows the tarot card reader a wide latitude. One of the most oustanding occult symbols providing endless research is the serpent. In its broad interpretation, it stands for sex or virile energy. When it is pictured biting its tail, it indicates eternity. When it appears with its head thrust upward, it means enlightenment. Also, if it is located at the brow of a person, it means enlightenment. However, should it appear in the region of the solar plexus, it signifies creative energies used for physical gratification alone.

Another example: the common meaning of *black* usually refers to something evil or unfortunate. On the other hand, it may symbolize a hidden facet—one not necessarily unfortunate. Then, take *torch:* in one pictograph it may indicate enlightenment or spirituality, while in another it may point to physical destruction—which could be either good or bad depending upon the associated topic matter.

Universal Symbols

Arrow: vengeance, unpleasant news
Black: evil, unfortunate, ignorance, deception
Bull: labor necessary for progress
Butterfly: immortality, pleasure
Chain: restrictions
Circle: eternity, spirit
Crescent: soul
Crocodile: cruelty
Cross: earth, matter, four elemental kingdoms
Cube: physical world
Cuirass: resistance
Darkness: sleep or death
Dove: peace
Dragon: powers of darkness and evil
Eagle: spiritual heights, sex
Earth: material world
Eyes: awareness
      bandaged; blinded, unprejudiced, inexperienced
Feet: understanding
Fish: gain
Five-pointed Star: a man or woman
      inverted; black magic
Flame: spirit
Flowers: virgin, happiness, love, good will
Goat: material and selfish ambitions
Gold: light
Hand: left; negative, feminine, receptive
      right; positive, masculine, executive
      pointed downward; physical
      pointed upward; spiritual
Hog: greed
Lamp: intelligence
Light: life and activity

Line: horizontal; passive, negative, feminine
    vertical; positive, masculine
    wavy; indecision
Lion: force, man's animal desires
Manna: spiritual nutriment
Moon: female
Pentagram: see Five-pointed Star
Pole Star: eternal truth
Pyramid: climax of earthly security
Scales: weighing good against evil, marriage
Scarab: immortality of the soul
Scorpion: selfishness
Scythe: harvest of earthly endeavors
Serpent: sex or virile energy
    biting its tail; enlightenment
    at the brow; enlightenment
    at the solar plexus; creative energies used for
        physical gratification alone
Sphinx: passage of time
Square: obstacles, struggle
Staff: progress through struggle, experience
Sun: male
Tau: virile force
Triangle: mind
Trine: luck, ease
Twelve stars: the zodiac
White: purity, fortunate, enlightenment
Young girl: purity

Here follow listings of key phrases for each of the 22 Major Arcana, the 40 Minor Arcana, and the 16 Court Arcana. Aside from the keyword of the decanate represented by each Minor Arcanum, and the common divinatory word for each of the Major and Minor Arcana, there is no special importance to the placement of the other key phrases in each list. Just above KEY PHRASES will be found the ASTROLOGICAL AS-SOCIATION which notes the symbolic principles upon which the key phrases are based.

MAJOR ARCANUM I

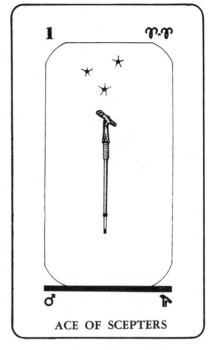

ACE OF SCEPTERS

THE MAGUS
ASTROLOGICAL ASSOCIATION:
Mercury
KEY PHRASES:
will or dexterity
gain through persistence
will power
mind over matter
triumph through analysis
faith in a higher power
acquire by effort
win over obstacles
justice through integrity
apply force with compassion
love of justice
take the initiative
changeable influences

ASTROLOGICAL ASSOCIATION:
Mercury, Aries, Mars
KEY PHRASES:
news of a business opportunity
activity
business activity of a mental
nature
business trip
aggressive intellectual pursuit
new activity on the job
new venture to benefit reputation
honor gained from mental
activity
scientific trends in business
business conference
analysis in personal affairs
defensive action to protect
honor
challenge demanding aggres-
sion
initiative taken
a telephone call

ACE OF CUPS

ASTROLOGICAL ASSOCIATION:
    Mercury, Cancer, Moon
KEY PHRASES:
a letter from a loved one
moods
emotional talk
mental quirks
journey out of sympathy
news about a new home
through study, meet a new
    love
travel concerned with domestic
    affairs
a sympathetic mental turn
a mood demanding analysis
analysis of affectional relations
love nature guided by intellect
misunderstood conversation
advice from a well-wisher

ACE OF COINS

ASTROLOGICAL ASSOCIATION:
    Mercury, Libra, Venus
KEY PHRASES:
a short journey
policy
money from the sale of a
    manuscript
cash in on artistic dexterity
scientific line of action
social contact for financial
    gain
writing or lecturing for money
friendly conversation
union of ideas
marriage for money
happy frame of mind
love of study
rewarding conversation in a
    social atmosphere
focus versatile talents
balance the budget
expenses for entertainment

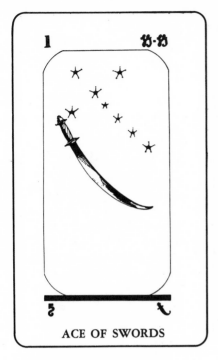

ACE OF SWORDS

MAJOR ARCANUM II

VEILED ISIS

ASTROLOGICAL ASSOCIATION:
Mercury, Capricorn,
Saturn

KEY PHRASES:
news of sickness or death
organization
trouble with your mail
death of an intellectual
    venture
struggle to gain organization
a depressed turn of mind
talk of a melancholy nature
opposition to your ideas
repression of news
delays in intellectual pursuits
difficulty in adjustment
faulty analysis
mental blocks
division of ideas
inability to talk fluently

ASTROLOGICAL ASSOCIATION:
Virgo

KEY PHRASES:
science
truth always wins
keep your intentions silent
don't cast your pearls before
    swine
choose your associates dis-
    criminately
sincerity unveils wisdom
follow your hunch
revelation through science
intellectual exchange
analyze your situation
an orderly work pattern
working environment
discreet service

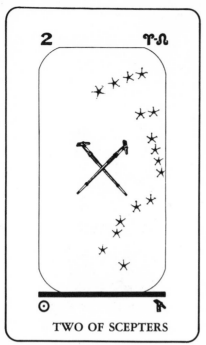

TWO OF SCEPTERS

TWO OF CUPS

ASTROLOGICAL ASSOCIATION:
Virgo, Leo, Sun
KEY PHRASES:
a business depending on
scientific methods
exaltation
watch your interests with
vigilance
obstacles resolved through
analysis
esteem of co-workers
pleasure in business
promotion at work
healthy frame of mind
success in business ventures
education for business
pioneering a new business
personal scientific adventure
prevent misunderstanding
with analysis
bring order into personal
habits
service for business reasons

ASTROLOGICAL ASSOCIATION:
Virgo, Cancer, Scorpio,
Moon, Pluto, Mars
KEY PHRASES:
a work of love
revelation
romantic impulses
love of home
scientific methods used in the
home
secret romance exposed
love of research
interest in mental pursuits
emotions guided by reason
affectionate demonstration
a perfect union
reciprocated love
passion controlled by reason
impulsive love affair

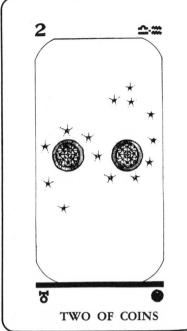

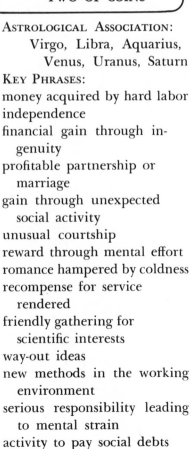

TWO OF COINS

TWO OF SWORDS

ASTROLOGICAL ASSOCIATION:
Virgo, Libra, Aquarius,
Venus, Uranus, Saturn

KEY PHRASES:
money acquired by hard labor
independence
financial gain through ingenuity
profitable partnership or
marriage
gain through unexpected
social activity
unusual courtship
reward through mental effort
romance hampered by coldness
recompense for service
rendered
friendly gathering for
scientific interests
way-out ideas
new methods in the working
environment
serious responsibility leading
to mental strain
activity to pay social debts

ASTROLOGICAL ASSOCIATION:
Virgo, Capricorn, Taurus,
Saturn, Venus

KEY PHRASES:
sickness through overwork
martyrdom
obstacles overcome by love
strength
mental development through
struggle
ultimate gain through perseverance
difficult road to success
reason influences superiors
triumph over obstacles
marital trouble
methodical patterns become
boring
trouble with possessions
practical approach toward
work
disappointment of a social
nature
responsibility to friends

MAJOR ARCANUM III

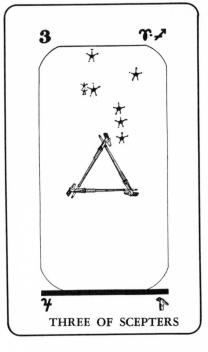

THREE OF SCEPTERS

ISIS UNVEILED

ASTROLOGICAL ASSOCIATION:
Libra
KEY PHRASES:
marriage or action
success in creative pursuits
mind over matter
thoughts are things
actions and reactions
union of minds
social activity
line of least resistance
unbalanced activity
indecision leads to sorrow
mental and social pursuits
friendly opposition
separation of ties

ASTROLOGICAL ASSOCIATION:
Libra, Aries, Sagittarius,
Mars, Jupiter
KEY PHRASES:
a business partnership
propaganda
jovial disposition
triumph over enemies
success in legal matters
take action for the future
business gains through social
activity
confidence in self
aggressive action
ultimate success
advertising activity
plan to raise prestige
active in church affairs
enthusiasm on the job

THREE OF CUPS

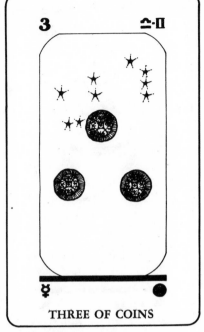

THREE OF COINS

ASTROLOGICAL ASSOCIATION:
   Libra, Cancer, Pisces,
   Moon, Neptune,
   Jupiter
KEY PHRASES:
a marriage for love
research
romantic activity
ideals realized through positive action
devotion to family
affections awakened
a warm friendship
danger of over-indulgence
faith in action
unbridled emotions
tendency to be oversensitive
prophetic dreams
acting upon illusion
artistic trends at work
psychic revelation

ASTROLOGICAL ASSOCIATION:
   Libra, Gemini, Venus,
   Mercury
KEY PHRASES:
a marriage for money
expiation
success in selling
gain through social activities
money gained by intellectual effort
profit from partnerships
compensation as a result of a business trip
money through the mail
remuneration from social intercourse
loose talk creates commotion
scattered interests defeat purpose
blend of social and mental activities
reward for creative endeavors
errors on the job

THREE OF SWORDS

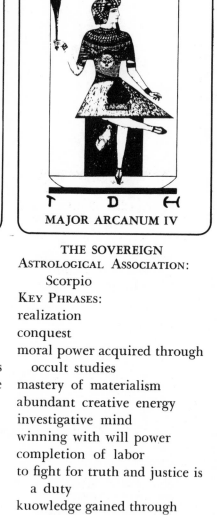

MAJOR ARCANUM IV

ASTROLOGICAL ASSOCIATION:
Libra, Capricorn, Virgo,
Saturn, Mercury
KEY PHRASES:
a law suit or a divorce
idealism
separation of mental concepts
organized activity to overcome
adversity
struggle in business
antagonistic talk attracts affliction
blend the ideal with the
practical
discord in business partnership
social split
plodding mental work
held down by responsibility
argument with a friend
false activity for social acclaim
underhanded methods in
business

THE SOVEREIGN
ASTROLOGICAL ASSOCIATION:
Scorpio
KEY PHRASES:
realization
conquest
moral power acquired through
occult studies
mastery of materialism
abundant creative energy
investigative mind
winning with will power
completion of labor
to fight for truth and justice is
a duty
kuowledge gained through
experience
triumph over obstacles
properly directed sex drive
confidence for proper de-
velopment

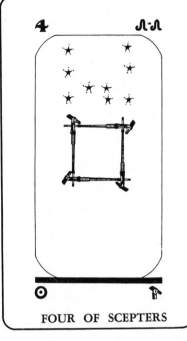

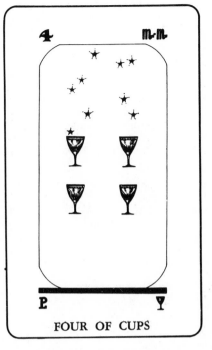

FOUR OF SCEPTERS

FOUR OF CUPS

ASTROLOGICAL ASSOCIATION:
Scorpio, Leo, Sun
KEY PHRASES:
a legacy
rulership
successful enterprise
honor gained through initiative
love dominates
promotion at work
influences by people in authority
reflected glory from children
good business credit
negotiations completed
applied will power attracts success
tensions in business bar progress
political maneuvers to gain realization
attain humility

ASTROLOGICAL ASSOCIATION:
Scorpio, Pluto, Mars
KEY PHRASES:
an increase in the family
resourcefulness
enduring love
great joys are in store for you
pleasure in group activity
a strong and lasting friendship
loving, parental care
lasting domestic harmony
emotional intuitiveness
affections realized
exposé of a revengeful plot
over emphasis of the emotions
drastic tactics to gain a point
active investigation brings results

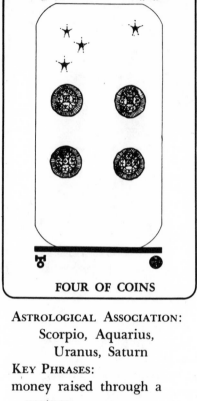

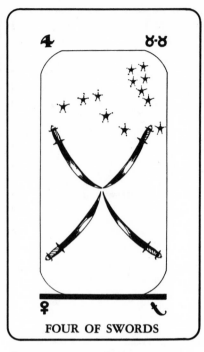

FOUR OF COINS

FOUR OF SWORDS

Astrological Association:
Scorpio, Aquarius,
Uranus, Saturn

Key Phrases:

money raised through a
partner

originality

gift from a friend

unexpected financial gain

reward for ingenuity

profit through invention

new avenue of realization

increase in wages

achievement through original
ideas

organization leads to profit

enduring possessions

mechanical or electrical conditions

planned activity for advancement

argument slows progress

Astrological Association:
Scorpio, Taurus, Venus

Key Phrases:

remorse for past action

determination

unfortunate romance

financial reverses

death of an artistic venture

hoarding of possessions

determination to overcome
obstacles

win through more give and
take

love gained through per-
severance

patience is rewarded

slow but sure climb

offending a friend

obstacles to realization

guard emotions against
negativeness

plodding persistence

132

MAJOR ARCANUM V

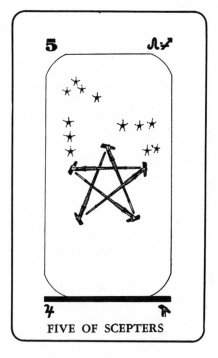

FIVE OF SCEPTERS

THE HIEROPHANT

ASTROLOGICAL ASSOCIATION:
Jupiter

KEY PHRASES:

religion or law

help through inspiration

realization from intelligence
and will

meditation brings enlightenment

success through good judgment

fortunate influences

strength from developing will
power

eventual success

triumph in legal matters

favors from professionals

good will leads to justice

materialism bars progress

avoid overindulgence

ASTROLOGICAL ASSOCIATION:
Jupiter, Leo, Sagittarius,
Sun

KEY PHRASES:

good fortune in business

reformation

social activity benefits job

gain through speculation

success of enterprise

theatrical success

business insight

child custody

inspiration through religion

practice faith

unsettled business practices

good will of customers and
clients

impulsive actions at work

rewards from a philosophical
attitude

faith in superiors

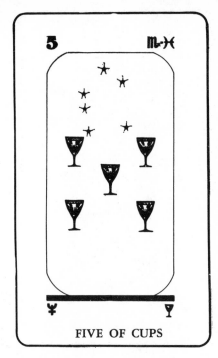

FIVE OF CUPS

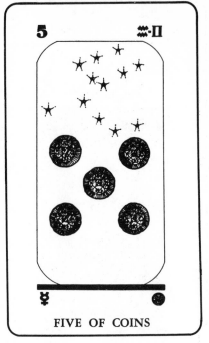

FIVE OF COINS

ASTROLOGICAL ASSOCIATION:
Jupiter, Scorpio, Pisces,
Pluto, Mars, Neptune

KEY PHRASES:
good fortune in love
responsibility
hold emotions in check
a deep-seated attachment
steadfast affections
benefit from hidden influences
check sensitivity with sound
  judgment
domestic illusions
fidelity in love
reinforce belief with facts
emotional responsibility attracted
realization of a dream
expand fixed ideas
rewarding psychic experience

ASTROLOGICAL ASSOCIATION:
Jupiter, Aquarius,
Gemini, Uranus,
Saturn, Mercury

KEY PHRASES:
abundant wealth
inspiration
spend wisely
reward from writing, teaching
  or lecturing
a trip for achievement
help through neighbors
study for future success
profitable contact
friendly assistance
money through original ideas
settlement of a lawsuit
expansion of the club's
  treasury
philosophical ideas attract
  wealth
overindulgence strains the
  budget
legal document in the mail

134

FIVE OF SWORDS

MAJOR ARCANUM VI

ASTROLOGICAL ASSOCIATION:
  Jupiter, Taurus, Virgo,
  Venus, Mercury
KEY PHRASES:
escape from danger
struggle
discrimination replaces impulsiveness
alertness pays off at the eleventh hour
overcome religious adversity
quarrels about possessions
obstacles overcome by faith
sickness due to financial worries
faith breaks the barrier
positive attitude helps prevent disease
benefit from reorganized working environment
gain through hard work
end of a legal battle
lifting of a restriction

THE TWO PATHS

ASTROLOGICAL ASSOCIATION:
  Venus
KEY PHRASES:
temptation
look beneath surface appearances
stick to your resolutions
make a firm decision
love of ease, comfort or luxury
resist sensualism
stabilize your emotions
probe for spiritual values
seek divine guidance
select your path with care
unfaithful affectionate nature
take a firm stand
friends surround you

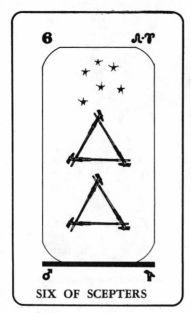

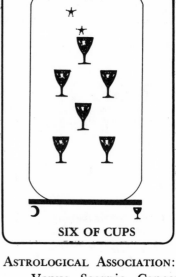

SIX OF SCEPTERS

SIX OF CUPS

ASTROLOGICAL ASSOCIATION:
Venus, Leo, Aries, Sun,
Mars

KEY PHRASES:
music, art, or drama
ambition
powerful love nature
seek moderation
avoid extreme measures in
business
promotion comes through the
ability to rule others
emphasize moderate aims and
goals
social activity to promote
business
balance pleasure with practicality
good manners win friends
rely on good taste
business of an artistic nature
the soft-sell brings more
success
focus energies to prevent
failure
control over aggressiveness at
work

ASTROLOGICAL ASSOCIATION:
Venus, Scorpio, Cancer,
Pluto, Mars, Moon

KEY PHRASES:
a love affair
attainment
beware the allurement of vice
check your hunches
carefully analyze your emotions
personal magnetism attracts
utilize your creative imagination
constructive activity overcomes
sensualism
fertility of ideas
resourcefulness brings harmony to the home
happy family event
firm will in affairs of the
heart
guard against changeable
loyalty
beneficial partnership

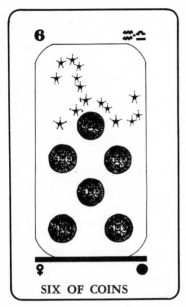

SIX OF COINS

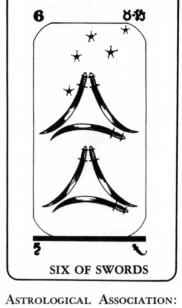

SIX OF SWORDS

ASTROLOGICAL ASSOCIATION:
  Venus, Aquarius, Libra,
  Uranus, Saturn
KEY PHRASES:
a social event
repression
the little things count
friendly criticism
psychology to win a point
profit from social affairs
reward through humanitarian
  activities
gain by original ideas
merger for money
love dominates material
  ambition
interest in world affairs
seek spiritual companionship
creative partnership for profit
be decisive when opportunity
  knocks

ASTROLOGICAL ASSOCIATION:
  Venus, Taurus, Capri-
  corn, Saturn
KEY PHRASES:
dissipation
mastership
budget your energies
struggle can lead to progress
news brings a temptation
a slow, steady climb to success
use talents to help others
antagonism of companions
scattered energies bring
  sorrow
trouble with your checking
  account
delays in affectional matters
temptation relating to business
a firm stand avoids dis-
  organization
organize your work

137

MAJOR ARCANUM VII

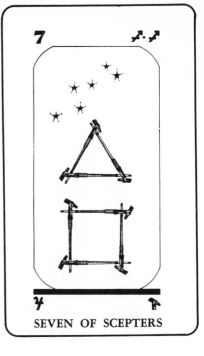

SEVEN OF SCEPTERS

THE CONQUEROR

ASTROLOGICAL ASSOCIATION:
　Sagittarius

KEY PHRASES:

victory

application of mental and
　physical powers

success through using intel-
　ligence

perfection attained by active
　effort

power to command others

vacation brings release

prompt and just decision

appraisal allows higher values

benefit by a philosophical
　approach

material condition conquered

circumvent red tape

zeal to serve mankind

travel stimulates enthusiasm

ASTROLOGICAL ASSOCIATION:
　Sagittarius, Jupiter

KEY PHRASES:

teaching or publishing

devotion

rely on your own judgment

protection from danger

benevolent influences sur-
　round you

keep aims on an ideal level

dissemination of constructive
　ideas

channel desires and control
　impulses

religious principles applied to
　business

personal philosophy wins
　popularity

business contacts in church
　groups

enthusiasm leads to promotion

benefit through professionals

pleasure on a business trip

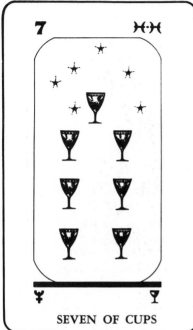

SEVEN OF CUPS

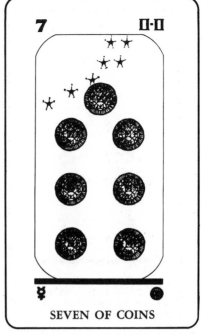

SEVEN OF COINS

ASTROLOGICAL ASSOCIATION:
Sagittarius, Pisces,
Neptune, Jupiter

KEY PHRASES:
a successful change of home
verity
ideal affectional exchange
love of social work
opportunity to dispel illusion
resolution of domestic discord
gain by unselfish love
devotion to family
sympathy for friends
compassion brings victory
truth revealed
inspired by a psychic ex-
perience
a deep feeling of contentment
faithful in love
misunderstanding corrected

ASTROLOGICAL ASSOCIATION:
Sagittarius, Gemini,
Mercury

KEY PHRASES:
money earned through a
journey
intuition
a profitable business trip
directed mental energy solves
a problem
profit from writing, publishing
or teaching
news leading to financial gain
discovery of a missing link
event involving radio or
television
intellectual victory
money from writing
cash in a letter
telegram about a financial opportunity
ESP experience
purchase of a new possession

SEVEN OF SWORDS

MAJOR ARCANUM VIII

THE BALANCE

ASTROLOGICAL ASSOCIATION:
Sagittarius, Virgo,
Mercury
KEY PHRASES:
danger through travel or
sports
achievement
progress follows conflict
faith overcomes physical afflictions
victory by hard work
positive thinking leads to
achievement
adverse publicity from co-
workers
ultimate gain through responsibilities
joy from pets
find solace in service
avoid pitfalls with discrimination
a call to service
positiveness weeds out negative thoughts
convert weaknesses into
strength
fight discord with faith

ASTROLOGICAL ASSOCIATION:
Capricorn
KEY PHRASES:
justice or equilibrium
develop a spirit of give and
take
conservativeness balanced by
originality
all work, no play makes Jack
a dull boy
moderation in all things
worry attracts discordant
events
directed thought banishes
crystallization
don't let things hang in the
balance
influence of a governmental
regulation
every action brings a reaction
curb the urge to dictate
serious exchange with
superiors
pleasure stimulates more
productivity

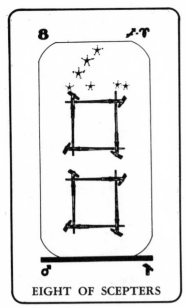

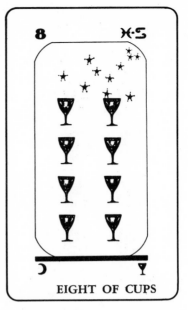

EIGHT OF SCEPTERS

EIGHT OF CUPS

ASTROLOGICAL ASSOCIATION:
  Capricorn, Sagittarius,
  Aries, Jupiter, Mars
KEY PHRASES:
a political appointment
exploration
business success through
  initiative
think before you act
action of a legal nature
personality affects reputation
promotion depending upon
  personal planning
transfer at work
responsibility of a business
  nature
new influences in working
  environment
rely on your own judgment
prestige in the professional
  world
self-confidence is needed

ASTROLOGICAL ASSOCIATION:
  Capricorn, Pisces, Cancer,
  Neptune, Jupiter,
  Moon
KEY PHRASES:
extravagance
self-sacrifice
blend the practical with the
  ideal
sacrifice for the home
misplaced emotion brings pain
don't let the heart rule the
  head
build a foundation for ideals
seek partner of similar
  emotional qualities
overpossessive in love
dominated by family res-
  ponsibilities
don't set your goals too high
uncontrolled sensitivity invites disaster
a lovers' quarrel
misleading psychic impression
caution in affectional matters

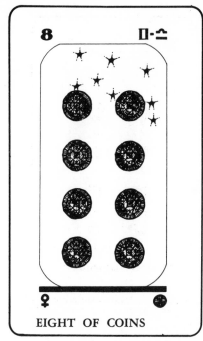

EIGHT OF COINS

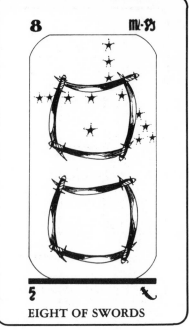

EIGHT OF SWORDS

ASTROLOGICAL ASSOCIATION:
Capricorn, Gemini, Libra,
Mercury, Venus

KEY PHRASES:
a costly law suit
fidelity
romance for money
flighty love affair
compensation from alimony
travel for love or money
compatible partnership
study for promotion
social activity financed for
political reasons
legal papers involving financial
transactions
marital litigations
perseverance at work brings
rewards
financial altercations with
neighbors
support from a friend

ASTROLOGICAL ASSOCIATION:
Capricorn, Virgo,
Mercury, Saturn

KEY PHRASES:
loss of honor, or business
failure
experience
life's limitations bring
strength
struggle to maintain balance
frustration results from con-
fining experiences
discontented with co-workers
fear of business failure
deficiencies detract from
progress
loss of prestige
added responsibility brings
worry
enthusiastic approach severs
limitation
disrupted routine of living
lessons to be learned
dissipation through overwork
positive thinking in the face of
adversity

MAJOR ARCANUM IX

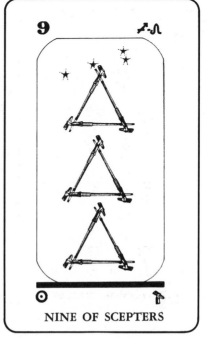

NINE OF SCEPTERS

THE SAGE

ASTROLOGICAL ASSOCIATION:
  Aquarius

KEY PHRASES:

wisdom or prudence

actions influenced by environment

discretion in all things

strength acquired through experimentation

silence in the face of argument

stability leads to accomplishment

knowledge from experience

a cautious psychological approach

foresight in humanitarian endeavors

analysis of hopes and wishes

blinded by outward appearances

know-how supports your endeavors

select associates wisely

ASTROLOGICAL ASSOCIATION:
  Aquarius, Sagittarius,
  Leo, Jupiter, Sun

KEY PHRASES:

wise and profitable friendship

illumination

happiness from children

success in entertainment business

reliable intuition

discretion in speculation

friends influence business

a scientific enterprise

business success depends upon prudence

knowledge of human nature leads to popularity

perseverance attracts promotion

original methods in business

arrogance has no place on the job

birth of a constructive idea

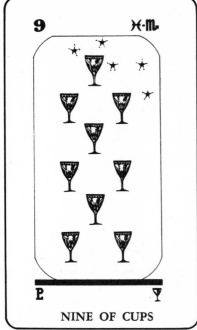

NINE OF CUPS

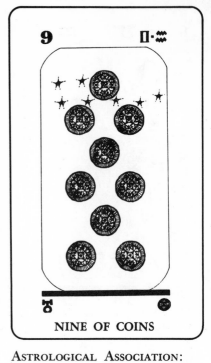

NINE OF COINS

ASTROLOGICAL ASSOCIATION:
Aquarius, Pisces, Scorpio,
Neptune, Jupiter,
Pluto, Mars

KEY PHRASES:

hopes will be realized

vicissitudes

passion supplanted by exalted
love

strong desire for affection

emotional stability

change in domestic affairs

a love of humanity

search for domestic harmony

alliance with a wise person

desirable outcome

spiritual love based on cooperation

wisdom in affairs of the heart

jealousy causes a rift

analysis of thoughts, feelings
and actions

ASTROLOGICAL ASSOCIATION:
Aquarius, Gemini, Mercury,
Uranus, Saturn

KEY PHRASES:

money spent on associates

reason

money gained through in-
ventiveness

sudden gain of fortune

common sense to increase income

benefit from relatives

change in frame of mind

further education to demand
a higher wage

unexpected gift from a friend

remuneration based upon
mental activity

gift from a neighbor

unexpected bill in the mail

sudden severance of a relationship

mental possessions endure
longer than physical

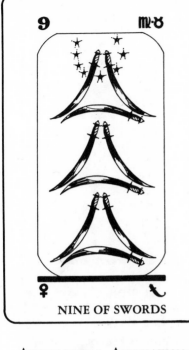

NINE OF SWORDS

MAJOR ARCANUM X

ASTROLOGICAL ASSOCIATION:
   Aquarius, Virgo, Taurus,
      Mercury, Venus
KEY PHRASES:
quarrel resulting in enmity
renunciation
avoid the trap of propaganda
poverty overcome by wisdom
sickness of a loved one
discordant working en-
   vironment
love overcomes arguments
loss of friendship
fixed mental attitudes bar
   achievement
letting go of old conditions
facts used as a blind
caution in human relations
energies wasted in argument
pleasant thoughts substituted
   for negativeness

THE WHEEL
ASTROLOGICAL ASSOCIATION:
   Uranus
KEY PHRASES:
change of fortune
patience will be rewarded
new conditions require
   adaptability
unexpected events occur
breaking of an old tie
a strong will defeats negativeness
dark before the dawn
recognize good from evil
guard against discordant
   environment
unconventional concepts
exercise caution to maintain
   equilibrium
be alert for opportunities
irritability and harshness
face change with courage

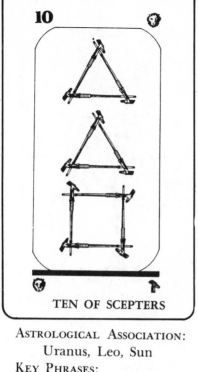

TEN OF SCEPTERS

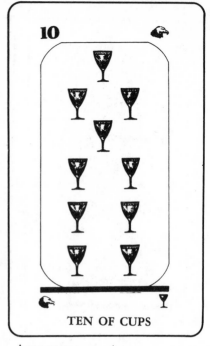

TEN OF CUPS

ASTROLOGICAL ASSOCIATION:
Uranus, Leo, Sun

KEY PHRASES:

an invention or discovery

new business methods

a change in status

alteration of working conditions

unconventional trends affect reputation

variety of personal activities

the new replaces the old

take initiative to maintain balance

a change in personality

sudden transfer at work

unexpected honor through the arts or sciences

different slant on entertainment

outdated principles applied to modern methods

effect of automation

ASTROLOGICAL ASSOCIATION:
Uranus, Scorpio, Pluto, Mars

KEY PHRASES:

an unconventional affectional interest

avoid emotional crossfire

inconstant emotions

unexpected ocean voyage

numerous and unusual friends

sudden love affair

reversal of feeling

forgotten taxes

uncommon love affair

revenge influences affections

an old love enters the life

target of sarcasm

sudden change in the home

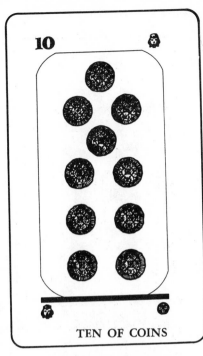

TEN OF COINS

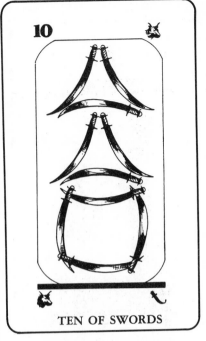

TEN OF SWORDS

ASTROLOGICAL ASSOCIATION:
Uranus, Aquarius,
Saturn

KEY PHRASES:

alternate financial loss and gain

give and receive reciprocally

unexpected air travel

inventiveness brings financial gain

mental inspiration

change of viewpoint

progressive gains

money gained through associates

gather and direct energies

shaky speculation

financial worries concerning a friend

new methods to control budget

wisdom from occult studies

ASTROLOGICAL ASSOCIATION:
Uranus, Taurus, Venus

KEY PHRASES:

sudden loss of employment

exposé leading to practical changes

static conditions in personal affairs

agitation upsets balance

unconventional actions

victim of eccentric afflictions

a series of gains and losses

faith helps in times of discouragement

do not abandon but keep trying

struggle leading to reform

hypersensitivity demands control

adaptation to enviroment

break stubborn habits

you could be your own worst enemy

MAJOR ARCANUM XI

MAJOR ARCANUM XII

THE ENCHANTRESS
ASTROLOGICAL ASSOCIATION:
  Neptune
KEY PHRASES:
force, spiritual power, or
  fortitude
develop and follow your
  intuition
moral force
advance with faith
reject temptations
hidden forces at work
overcome evil with good
accomplish your duties without hesitation
obstacles are more imaginary
  than real
confusion and lack of force
success demands organization
fear defeats purpose
facing reality clarifies nebulous influences

THE MARTYR
ASTROLOGICAL ASSOCIATION:
  Pisces
KEY PHRASES:
sacrifice or expiation
forgive your enemies
the material world may
  dominate the soul
wasted effort
ebbing of life forces
disappointment
choose after careful consideration
worry tears down results
emotional sorrow
over idealistic
stirring of creative urges
apply the imagination
material temptation con-
  quered
giving without thought of
  recompense

148

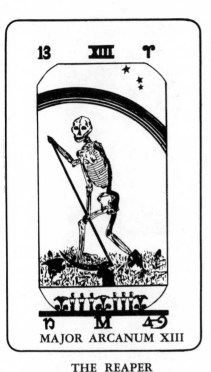

MAJOR ARCANUM XIII

MAJOR ARCANUM XIV

THE REAPER

ASTROLOGICAL ASSOCIATION:
Aries

KEY PHRASES:

death or transformation
a new venture
guard impulsiveness
immortality is promised
death of selfishness
rise above materialism
faced with a new door
youthful viewpoint
energetic mental activity
end of a situation
influence of mechanical
  gadgets
strong competition
new creative trends

THE ALCHEMIST

ASTROLOGICAL ASSOCIATION:
Taurus

KEY PHRASES:

regeneration or temperance
diligence to reach goal
man and woman united
money obtained from plod-
  ding effort
keep company with har-
  monious people
partnership in unselfish
  service
stubbornness bars the way
a perfect union
moderate spending
passionless love
possessiveness repels your
  heart's desire
work together in harmony
patience is rewarded

MAJOR ARCANUM XV

MAJOR ARCANUM XVI

THE BLACK MAGICIAN

ASTROLOGICAL ASSOCIATION:
Saturn

KEY PHRASES:

fatality or black magic

selfishness leads to loneliness
and poverty

more is won through love than
hate

material ambitions should be
balanced with mental
pursuits

cruelty hurts only the giver

overcome pride and self-
interest

delays avoided by careful
planning

discontent invites depression

deceptive and disintegrative
activity

undermining influences at
work

greed brings eventual un-
happiness

replace coldness with warmth

secret and hidden trends

take pleasure in overcoming
handicaps

THE LIGHTNING

ASTROLOGICAL ASSOCIATION:
Mars

KEY PHRASES:

accident or catastrophe

you reap what you sow

do not dissipate energies

fight for high principles

save energy for constructive
pursuits

release undesirable instincts

constructive effort dominates
evil influences

impulsiveness attracts failure

love paralyzes evil

need of undaunted courage

irritability invites mistakes

develop self to avert danger

modify inner conflicts

applied creative energies

THE STAR	THE MOON

ASTROLOGICAL ASSOCIATION:
   Gemini

KEY PHRASES:

truth, hope or faith

do not limit yourself

distinguish reality from
   illusion

cultivate a positive attitude

truth demands a blending of
   heart and mind

select a goal and stick to it

follow projects through to
   completion

replace restlessness with faith

search for the truth

relationship with neighbors

effect of the spoken word

privately expressed ideas

overcoming problems
   strengthens character

ASTROLOGICAL ASSOCIATION:
   Cancer

KEY PHRASES:

deception, false friends or
   secret foes

hostile mind attracts enemies

silence is golden

choose companions carefully

place yourself in a better environment

energetic action overcomes
   lethargy

look beneath the glamour of
   appearance

temper your emotions with
   analysis

too much sympathy empha-
   sizes discord

enemies veiled in the grab of
   flattery

constant vacillation reaps no
   harvest

abuse of occult powers invites destruction

strive for harmony in the
   home

MAJOR ARCANUM XIX

MAJOR ARCANUM XX

THE SUN

ASTROLOGICAL ASSOCIATION:
Leo

KEY PHRASES:

happiness or joy

no one can hurt you but
yourself

guard the sacredness of
marriage

infidelity leads to unhappiness

align physical, mental, and
spiritual goals

moderate your desires

children compensate for
material hardships

rewards through unselfish
love

sacrifice for the family

devotion to peace and
harmony

a happy marriage

self organization attracts contentment

a circle of love protects you

THE SARCOPHAGUS

ASTROLOGICAL ASSOCIATION:
Moon

KEY PHRASES:

awakening or resurrection

nothing is more permanent
than change

banish idleness with action

an end is also a beginning

the turning of a page in life

rise above emotional turmoil

establish new personal relationships

death is but a transition

passing of an old condition
leads to a new one

through perception there is
awareness

broaden your mentality

timing is of the essence

shun ease and comfort for
progress

reversal of emotions

152

MAJOR ARCANUM XXI

MAJOR ARCANUM XXII

THE ADEPT
ASTROLOGICAL ASSOCIATION:
Sun

KEY PHRASES:
success or attainment
application of will power
know yourself to know success
utilize your creative imagination
strength from harmonious
actions
take pleasure in your work
perfection through persistence
good will of those in authority
synchronize body, mind and
emotions
celebrities as friends
masculine methods
overbearing actions of
superiors
attainment through
perseverance

THE MATERIALIST
ASTROLOGICAL ASSOCIATION:
Pluto

KEY PHRASES:
failure, folly, mistake, or
spirituality
indiscretion can be your
downfall
material life over emphasized
wisdom prevents obsession
a slave to desire
group cooperation
coerced by others
doubt destroys faith
suffering follows sin
hope through prayer
blinded by selfish interests
rewards from community
activity
realization of humanitarian
efforts

153

KING OF SCEPTERS

A man of an
Aries temperament

KING OF SWORDS

A man of a
Taurus temperament

KING OF COINS

A man of a
Gemini temperament

KING OF CUPS

A man of a
Cancer temperament

QUEEN OF SCEPTERS

A woman of a
Leo temperament

QUEEN OF SWORDS

A woman of a
Virgo temperament

QUEEN OF COINS

A woman of a
Libra temperament

QUEEN OF CUPS

A woman of a
Scorpio temperament

YOUTH OF SCEPTERS

A youth of a
Sagittarian temperament

YOUTH OF SWORDS

A youth of a
Capricorn temperament

YOUTH OF COINS

A youth of an
Aquarian temperament

YOUTH OF CUPS

A youth of a
Pisces temperament

HORSEMAN OF SCEPTERS

HORSEMAN OF SWORDS

Thoughts of business

Upright: thoughts advantageous to the querent

Reversed: thoughts opposed to his business interests

Thoughts of enmity, strife and sickness

Upright: thoughts devoted to the querent's defense and promotion

Reversed: plans and desires for the querent's downfall

HORSEMAN OF COINS

HORSEMAN OF CUPS

Thoughts of health or money

Upright: thoughts to increase querent's prosperity

Reversed: thoughts which plot unfair financial advantage of the querent

Thoughts of love and affection

Upright: sincere thoughts to the querent's advantage

Reversed: deceit or opposition to the true affectional desires

Part IV

ASTROLOGICAL SYMBOLISM

$\mathcal{T}$his section was designed to help the reader select additional meanings indicated by the astrological symbolism appearing on the tarot cards. Everything in the universe is ruled by an astrological sign or planet. Consulting these categories will reveal unlimited associations. For ready reference, this information is listed under each sign and planet in the following classifications.

Appearance and Body Structure

As a rule, Court cards depict people, but in addition, other cards may also indicate people. In either case, the astrological symbolism on a card gives a clue to personal description. Each sign and each planet is commonly associated with certain physical characteristics. Therefore, a reference to these physical descriptions will prove invaluable.

When a reader sees a card in the past of a spread, he can describe the person from the sign or planet appearing on that card. Once the querent recognizes this person, it will assist the reader to tell how past events led to the present.

In like manner, when a person card appears in the future, the reader will be able to describe that person. Whether a person card appears in the past, present, or future, knowing his indicated physical characteristics will assist the querent to eliminate one or more persons he may have in mind.

Temperament

Here are given the frame of mind or type of mental reaction characteristic of individuals identified with each of the twelve signs and the ten planets. This section may be consulted to determine the temperament of people in the same manner as the Appearance and Body Structure classification is used.

It should be remembered that a person not born under the sign of Aries may still have strong Aries traits if he has planets in Aries or Aries rising. This can only be determined by erecting his personal birth chart.

But even when a person is born under Aries, he will not always express every Aries trait. This is because his Aries expression is modified by other factors in his horoscope in addition to his conditioning.

In any case, this classification covers the highlights of his personality, his best and worst traits, how to appeal to him, and what he needs to do to raise his own level of expression to attract success.

Personal Interests

A person has a limited amount of energy to utilize in expressing himself. It is natural for him to channel his energies into definite activities. He would feel unfulfilled if his basic urges were not satisfied. This classification gives the specific directions in which personal interests and affairs are focused.

Occupations

Certain signs and certain planets stand for natural aptitudes and desires for specific occupations. However, no sign or planet exclusively rules any given occupation. Occupations listed here are those most strongly identified with the sign and planet under which they appear.

Significant Associations

In the previous classifications, certain vibratory rates corresponding to signs and planets were associated with individuals. Here we have expanded this principle to include objects in the environment.

Everything has an astrological rulership commonly called its astrological signature. When a group of objects are all ruled by a particular sign or planet, they each have the same astrological signature and express the same quality of energy. Given here are numbers, colors, gems, and herbs bearing the astrological signature for each sign and planet.

Often the content of a question will allow the reader to use this classification. For instance, these environmental influences may be associated with to accentuate a desired vibration or may be avoided if the astrological signature is undesirable. Mental alchemists employ them as antidotes for discord.

Environmental Factors

Environment should be considered in every spread, as it is often importantly associated with the querent's question. When parts of the city or the home are involved, the zodiacal signs designate definite areas. The signs also signify climate or land. Other environmental factors, such as inanimate objects and people, are depicted by the planets. These associations of the twelve signs and the ten planets to environmental factors will be found in this classification.

Cities of the World

To establish the rulership of a city, some authorities have selected the Sun-Sign, some the Ascending-Sign, some the Midheaven-Sign, and some the incorporation date or founding date. In this work, to standardize the rulerships of cities, we have adopted Sepharial's system of geodetic equivalents.

Starting at Greenwich, England, Sepharial matched the 360 degrees of geographical longitude with the 360 degrees of zodiacal longitude. As there are twelve signs of the zodiac, each embracing 30 degrees, a thirty-degree segment of geographical longitude was associated with one sign of the zodiac. He correlated the geographical area from Zero to 30 degrees east with the sign Aries in the heavens. Therefore, from 30 to 60 degrees east longitude corresponds to the sign Taurus, and so forth around the world.

Rulerships of countries are not given, because when geodetic equivalents are employed, a country often falls into two or more geodetic areas. In this classification, the countries and states in which the cities are located appear alphabetically.

United States of America

The sign rulerships of the 50 United States of America were determined from the sign the Sun was in on the date each state was admitted into the Union.

World Affairs

This classification will give assistance in the reading of spreads concerning city, state, national, or international affairs. It may also be consulted when questions of public interest arise.

The community, national and international activities corresponding to each sign of the zodiac are given. And under each planet, this classification furnishes the key emphasis on thought, business and politics.

Personal Ability

Because planets symbolize ability and signs designate motivation, personal ability is not listed under signs of the zodiac. To learn if a prospective employee has needed qualifications, or which member of a group has the necessary talent to handle a particular duty, and the like, this section will prove useful.

The following tables will aid the tarot card reader to quickly identify astrological symbolism.

Sun-Sign Dates

Aries	March 21—April 19	Libra	Sept. 23—Oct. 22
Taurus	April 20—May 20	Scorpio	Oct. 23—Nov. 21
Gemini	May 21—June 20	Sagittarius	Nov. 22—Dec. 21
Cancer	June 21—July 22	Capricorn	Dec. 22—Jan. 19
Leo	July 23—Aug. 22	Aquarius	Jan. 20—Feb. 18
Virgo	Aug. 23—Sept. 22	Pisces	Feb. 19—March 20

ZODIACAL SIGNS

♈ – ARIES	♎ – LIBRA
♉ – TAURUS	♏ – SCORPIO
♊ – GEMINI	♐ – SAGITTARIUS
♋ – CANCER	♑ – CAPRICORN
♌ – LEO	♒ – AQUARIUS
♍ – VIRGO	♓ – PISCES

PLANETS

☉ – SUN	♃ – JUPITER
☽ – MOON	♄ – SATURN
☿ – MERCURY	♅ – URANIUS
♀ – VENUS	♆ – NEPTUNE
♂ – MARS	♇ – PLUTO

ZODIACAL SIGNS AND THEIR PLANETARY RULERS

♈ – ♂	♎ – ♀
♉ – ♀	♏ – ♇ AND ♂
♊ – ☿	♐ – ♃
♋ – ☽	♑ – ♄
♌ – ☉	♒ – ♅ AND ♄
♍ – ☿	♓ – ♆ AND ♃

Following is a listing in detail by personal characteristics, significant associations, environmental factors, etc., for each astrologic symbol or connotation as previously mentioned.

ARIES

APPEARANCE AND BODY STRUCTURE: Middle stature, spare, strong body, bushy eyebrows, dark hair, rather swarthy. Rules head and face, upper jaw, the cerebrum, upper hemisphere of the brain.

TEMPERAMENT: An Aries person expresses a fiery will, executive ability, and a dauntless pioneering spirit. He is ambitious, enterprising, forceful, combative, self-willed, independent and active. He loves to be in command and resents being confined or dictated to. Precedent or environment affect him little.

Being headstrong and aggressive, under stress his fiery temper is ignited. Because he becomes passionately concerned about things, when opposed he often becomes quarrelsome. Once he has taken up arms in behalf of a cause, he is very difficult to dissuade. On the other hand, in his work of construction, he marshals his creative power and original thought, which is always guided by intellect.

The need of combat or the zest of competition brings out the best in an Aries, because he constantly strives for personal leadership. His optimism often plunges him into projects that are too big for him to cope with. He should avoid having too many irons in the fire at one time. He instinctively rushes into controversy before he has had time to evaluate the situation. But because he is a good mixer and is bright and lively, he finds it easy to talk his way out of any corner.

In his desire to express his best quality of leadership, he is apt to become too bossy, his worst quality. Therefore, he should learn to direct his energies and concentrate his powers of leadership constructively—not interfering in the affairs of others.

PERSONAL INTERESTS: Affairs concerned with personal appearance, temperament, health, vitality, length of life, personal ability.

OCCUPATIONS: Athletes, barbers, diamond cutters, firemen, guards, hardware salesmen, iron workers, manufacturers, masseurs, metallurgical engineers, optometrists, physical therapists, physiotherapists, propulsion technicians, sheet metal workers, soldiers, stationary engineers, surgeons, thermodynamicists, tool designers, welders.

SIGNIFICANT ASSOCIATIONS: Number 13. Letter M. Color light red. Tone high C. Talismanic gem amethyst. Such stones as ochre, brimstone and red stones of all kinds. Such herbs as hemp, mustard, broom, holly, dock, thistle, fern, garlic, onions, nettles, radishes, poppies, peppers and rhubarb.

ENVIRONMENTAL FACTORS: Country: sparsely settled, moderately high and rugged. Climate: hot, dry. Land: where pebbles and boulders are numerous, fields that are freshly plowed. City: the manufacturing district, hardware stores, repair garages and auto service stations. Home: doorways, roof, tool-rooms, furniture tops, and things made of iron and steel.

CITIES OF THE WORLD: ALBANIA, Tirana. ALGERIA, Algiers, Fort Laperrine. ANGOLA, Luanda. AUSTRIA, Vienna. BELGIUM, Brussels. BULGARIA, Sofia. CHAD, Fort Lamy. CONGO, Leopoldville. CONGO REPUBLIC: Brazzaville. CZECHOSLOVAKIA, Prague. DAHOMEY, Porto Novo. DENMARK, Copenhagen. EGYPT, Alexandria. ESTONIA, Tallinn. FINLAND, Helsinki. FRANCE, Lyon, Marseille, Paris. GABON, Libreville. GERMANY, Berlin, Essen, Munich. GREECE, Athens. HOLLAND, Amsterdam. HUNGARY, Budapest. ITALY, Florence, Genoa, Milan, Rome. LATVIA, Riga. LITHUANIA, Kaunas, NAGER, Nismey. NIGERIA, Ibaban, Lagos.

NORWAY, Oslo. POLAND, Warsaw. ROMANIA, Bucharest. SOUTH AFRICA, Capetown, East London, Johannesburg, Port Elizabeth. SWEDEN, Stockholm. SWITZERLAND, Berne. TUNISIA, Tunis. TURKEY, Istanbul. YUGOSLAVIA, Belgrade.

UNITED STATES OF AMERICA: None.

WORLD AFFAIRS: National matters concerned with the people of a country: their disposition, health and personal affairs as distinct from their foreign interests.

TAURUS

APPEARANCE AND BODY STRUCTURE: Short, thick set, dull complexion, large mouth, dark hair and eyes. Rules the neck, throat, ears, palate, tonsils, cerebellum, the occipital region, larynx, pharynx and vocal cords.

TEMPERAMENT: A Taurus person is plodding, practical and self-reliant. A persistent and untiring worker with enormous reserve energy, he can wait a long time for plans to mature. He does not intrude upon others, nor does he bow to their opinions. He would rather use his own pronounced powers of discrimination. He is strongly attracted to money and expresses himself by its use.

Because he is naturally quiet and thoughtful, he is often secretive. This manner covers a certain sense of timidity. Even though he is slow to anger, once aroused, he is furious and violent. But when he cools off, he is sullen and reserved and becomes a relentless enemy. On the other hand, if he befriends you, he will be a friend for life. Because he dislikes changing personal relationships, he is apt to become overpossessive.

The Taurus person is careful and steadfast in mind and habits. A lover of routine, he dislikes changing his methods in any way. He is thorough in all that he does and takes great joy in perfecting the small details. He cannot be hurried, pushed or frightened out of his deliberate pace. If he is, he becomes stubborn and immovable. He is obedient to his employer and persistent to the end. He retreats from new ventures, for he dislikes taking the initiative. Rather, he is conservative in both thought and action. His best quality is stability, and he can be trusted with other people's possessions.

The character trait which detracts most from his success is stubbornness. Living in an everchanging world, he needs to learn adaptability so that new opportunities will not pass him by. By so doing, he will be better equipped to gain the possessions which he needs to make his life tolerable.

PERSONAL INTERESTS: Affairs concerned with wealth, personal property, profit and loss, cash, fruits of labor in terms of ease and possessions.

OCCUPATIONS: Bankers, bank tellers, cabinet makers, carpet layers, cashiers, commercial artists, farmers, financiers, geologists, industrial designers, landscapers, sales agents, singers, surveyors, tile setters, treasurers.

SIGNIFICANT ASSOCIATIONS: Number 14. Letter N. Color dark yellow. Tone low E. Talismanic gem moss agate. Such stones as alabaster, white opaque stones and white coral. Such herbs as daisies, dandelion, myrtle, gourds, flax, lilies, larkspur, spinach, moss.

ENVIRONMENTAL FACTORS: Country: low, level, without brush or woods. Climate: cold, dry. Land: where seed has been planted. City: banks, safes, vaults, cash registers and places where money and securities are kept. Home: store rooms, trunks, strong-boxes, bank books, checkbooks, purses and wallets.

CITIES OF THE WORLD: ANGLO EGYPT SUDAN, Khartoum. ARABIA, Mecca, Riyadh. EGYPT, Cairo, Port Said. ETHIOPIA, Addis Ababa. IRAN, Tehran. IRAQ, Baghdad. ISREAL, Jerusalem. MADAGASCAR, Tananarive. SOMALILAND, Mogadiscio. SOUTH AFRICA, Durban, Lourenco, Marques. SOVIET UNION, Baku, Kharkov, Leningrad, Molotov, Moscow, Rostov, Stalingrad, Tbilisi. TANGANYIKA, Zanzibar. TURKEY, Ankara.

UNITED STATES OF AMERICA: Louisiana, Maryland, Minnesota.

WORLD AFFAIRS: Associated with national matters dependent upon the wealth and personal property of the people, the national treasury, banks, non-speculative bonds and securities, financial transactions, and places where money and securities are handled.

GEMINI

APPEARANCE AND BODY STRUCTURE: Tall, long arms, light complexion, brown hair, quick in action. Rules the shoulders, arms, hands, bronchi and lungs.

TEMPERAMENT: A Gemini person exerts considerable initiative. Endowed with a versatile nature, he is usually interested in several things at once, and often changes his occupation. He has a fondness for learning, is changeable, sensitive, skillful and intuitive. Due to his restlessness and his insatiable curiosity, he is constantly seeking the "why" of things.

With a well-developed intuition and reason, he makes a good teacher. He is fond of all kinds of knowledge. He possesses wonderful powers of mental expansion and a constant flow of ideas expressed through conversation and writing. Energetic and enterprising, he quickly acquires skill with his hands, often following more than one occupation at the same time. Instead of changing occupations, he should use his mental agility to discover new methods in the one he has chosen. His difficulty lies in concentrating his energies long enough in one channel to make it a success.

Because he must constantly express himself in some way, he is at his best when his intellect has full scope. He is not bound so much by material motives as by the desire for mental expression. At times, he becomes long-winded and may talk so much about insignificant details that important information is lost.

His best quality is versatility, and he can do many things well. Therefore, he should take care to evaluate his personal activities properly. Unless he does so, his worst quality, change-ableness, takes over. Then a constantly changing view-point could leave him without convictions, and he would likely run from disagreeableness. To counteract this, he should budget his energies so that a scattering of his forces will not dissipate his true talents.

PERSONAL INTERESTS: Affairs concerned with brothers and sisters, neighbors, writing, short trips, correspondence, education, private studies, science, news, rumors, cousins, newspapers, periodicals, messengers, land transportation and thoughts.

OCCUPATIONS: Automobile mechanics, bookbinders, book-keepers, bus drivers, business machine repairmen, cab drivers, canvassers, clerk-typists, desk clerks, elevator operators, graphologists, IBM operators, librarians, mail carriers, manicurists, mechanical engineers, medical record librarians, messengers, navigators, newsboys, newspaper reporters, occupational therapists, office boys, office machine operators, photoengravers, porters, printers, proofreaders, radio operators, railroad men, service station attendants, shipping and receiving clerks, solicitors, stenographers, technical writers, telephone repairmen, ticket agents, truck drivers, typesetters, weather observers, writers.

SIGNIFICANT ASSOCIATIONS: Number 17. Letters F, Ph, P. Color light violet. Tone high B. Talismanic gem beryl. Such stones as are striped. Herbs such as madder, tansy, vervain, woodbine, yarrow, meadow-sweet, privet and dog-grass.

ENVIRONMENTAL FACTORS: Country: thickly settled, a city or town, moderately high. Climate: temperate, where the wind blows. Land: rather rolling and covered with grass, small trees and shrubs; or where crops have just come through the ground. City: railroad yards, street cars, buses, post offices, telephone and telegraph systems. Home: halls, windows, telephone, writing desk, library, study, mailbox, files, typewriter, magazine rack, letters, newspapers.

CITIES OF THE WORLD: AFGHANISTAN, Kabul. CELON, Columbo. CHINA, Soche, Tihwa. INDIA, Ahmedabad, Bangalore, Benares, Bombay, Calcutta, Delhi, Hyderabad, Kozhikode, Madres, Nagpur, Nepal, Srinagar. PAKISTAN, Karachi, Lahore. SOVIET UNION, Balkhash, Dikson, Omsk, Salekhard, Samarkand, Stalinsk, Sverdlovsk, Tashkent.

UNITED STATES OF AMERICA: Arkansas, Kentucky, Rhode Island, South Carolina, Tennessee, West Virginia, Wisconsin.

WORLD AFFAIRS: Associated with national matters dependent upon transportation, railroads, roads, motor buses, automobiles, local airplane traffic, local traffic in general, printing, newspapers, magazines, other periodicals. Literary work, intellectual activity, the thoughts of the people, neighboring countries.

CANCER

APPEARANCE AND BODY STRUCTURE: Middle height, upper parts larger, small mouth and face, pale, milky eyes. Rules lower part of lungs, breasts, diaphragm and stomach.

TEMPERAMENT: A Cancer person is subject to whims, moods and varying changes. Because it is easy for him to alter his own position, he dislikes being confined in a single environment. He is not usually physical, but he is intensely active assimilating and redistributing the impressions he absorbs from his environment. Due to his extreme sensitiveness and mediumistic tendencies, environment is most important in his life.

Even though he is timid and retiring, he has a strong desire to carry out his own ideas in his own way. What he lacks in aggressiveness, he makes up with tenacity. He possesses good reflective powers which often tend toward day-dreaming and fantasy thinking. His moods and yearnings are expressed pronouncedly.

The best way to appeal to him is through kindness, sympathy and praise. Because he tends to absorb all the conditions he contacts, he should choose his associates carefully. Noisy, boisterous and crude people rub him the wrong way, and he is distressed in a dog-eat-dog world.

Whether a man or a woman, a Cancer person is strongly domestic due to his protective instincts. Even though he has a gentle nature most of the time, he will fight for the underdog. The fear of ridicule is torture to him and prevents him from asserting himself to advantage. But when he has a friend, idea, or purpose to cling to, he does so with utmost patience. His best quality is persistence.

When he feels he has been slighted, he often becomes touchy—his worst quality. Unpleasant news upsets him. He needs to absorb the idea that people are generally sympathetic and friendly, and learn to adapt to those who do not seem to have these qualities. In this manner, he will not repel the very opportunities he most desires when they are presented.

PERSONAL INTERESTS: Affairs concerned with the home, environment, father, domestic life, inherited tendencies, real estate, hidden things, lands, mines, houses, crops, the grave, cities and towns.

OCCUPATIONS: Baby sitters, bakers, biochemists, caretakers, cooks, custodians, foresters, gardeners, grocers, historians, laundry workers, merchants, meteorologists, milkmen, obstetricians, real estate agents, restaurant managers.

SIGNIFICANT ASSOCIATIONS: Number 18. Letters Sh, Ts, Tz. Color light green. Tone high F. Talismanic gem emerald. Such stones as are soft and white, including selenite and chalk. Herbs such as water lilies, rushes, cucumbers, squashes, melons, and water plants generally.

ENVIRONMENTAL FACTORS: Country: along the ocean beach, or where small active streams flow. Climate: wet, cool. Land: rich, sandy loam in creek or river bottom, or near the ocean. City:

reservoirs, water pipes and hydrants, running water, hotels and the main residential district. Home: bathroom, laundry, living room, washing machine, liquids, swimming pool, yard, and water meter.

CITIES OF THE WORLD: AUSTRALIA, Albany, Carnarvon, Fremantle, Geraldton, Berth. BURMA, Mandalay, Rangoon. CHINA, Canton, Changsha, Chunking, Foochow, Hanchow, Hankow, Hongkong, Kuming, Lanchow, Nanking, Peiping, Sian, Tientsin. MALAYA, Singapore. MONGOLIA, Ulan-Bator-Khoto. SOVIET UNION, Kirensk, Nordic. SUMATRA, Padang. THAILAND, Bangkok. VIETNAM, Hanoi, Saigon.

UNITED STATES OF AMERICA: Idaho, New Hampshire, Virginia, Wyoming.

WORLD AFFAIRS: Associated with national matters dependent upon the land, the homes of the people, buildings, hotels, roominghouses; the weather, agriculture, crops on the ground, mining; the political party that is out of power but opposed to the ruling party.

LEO

APPEARANCE AND BODY STRUCTURE: Breadth and size to stature, large head, light hair, ruddy complexion. Rules the spine, back and heart.

TEMPERAMENT: A Leo person possesses a strong determination to rise. He is forceful, candid, and loves honors and high offices. He strives to rule through strength and stability rather than through his alertness and activity. His actions spring from his emotions rather than from his intellect. His ideas are large and majestic, and he despises petty effort. In trying to gain his high ideals he often overreaches. In his ambition, he is impulsive, passionate and daring.

He is noted for his courage, for the strength of his physical constitution, and for his recuperative powers. He is honest, fearless, magnanimous, generous to his friends, and sympathetic. Because he is regal, proud, and dignified, he is a natural ruler of others.

He places great faith and trust in other people, who usually respond to this faith by trying to live up to his expectations. Being sympathetic and warmhearted, he does not demand the impossible of subordinates. His best quality is kindness.

If his thirst for personal glory carries him too far, he becomes domineering, his worst quality. Sometimes he feels he should have a higher position of importance in life even though he may be incapable of handling it. Regardless of his position, he should express his splendid organizational traits kindly no matter where he finds himself. This will build a channel through which the highest glories and the warmest friendships will come to him.

PERSONAL INTERESTS: Affairs concerned with children, pleasure, speculation, amusements, offspring, love affairs, courtship, theatres, all places of amusement, gambling, hazards, schools, parties and entertainment.

OCCUPATIONS: Actors, cartoonists, entertainers, fashion designers, foremen, jewelers, package designers, politicians, stock brokers, supervisors, theatre managers, ushers.

SIGNIFICANT ASSOCIATIONS: Number 19. Letter G. Color light orange. Tone high D. Talismanic gem ruby. Such stones as the chrysolite, hyacinth and soft yellow minerals. Herbs such as camomile, daffodil, cowslip, anise, eglantine, fennel, eyebright, dill, lavender, poppy, yellow lily, marigold, St. John's wort, mistletoe, pimpernel, parsley and garden mint.

ENVIRONMENTAL FACTORS: Country: rather low, with level stretches tending to desert conditions. Climate: hot, dry. Land: wild, or kept for the purpose of sport or amusement. City: theatres, schools, playgrounds, parks, and places of amusement. Home: the nursery and places where children congregate, furnace room, places where pots and kettles are kept, party supplies, irons, cigarette lighters, stoves, fireplaces and all places where fire is used.

CITIES OF THE WORLD: AUSTRALIA, Adelaide, Alice Springs, Broome Cairns, Cloncurry, Daly Waters, Darwin, Kalgoorlie, Melbourne, Townsville. CHINA, Shanghai. JAPAN, Yokohama. KOREA, Pusan, Seoul. MANCHURIA, Mukden. MANILA, Quezon City. MINDANAO, Davoa. NEW GUINEA, Hollandia, Madang, Port Moresby. SOVIET UNION, Aldan, Okhotak, Tiksi, Verkhovansk, Vladivostok, Yakutak. TASMANIA, Hobart.

UNITED STATES OF AMERICA: Colorado, Hawaii, Missouri, New York.

WORLD AFFAIRS: National matters associated with entertainment and the motion picture industry, theatres, other places of amusement, the birth rate, speculation, the stock market and stock exchange, ambassadors from foreign countries, children and places where children congregate, such as schools and colleges.

VIRGO

APPEARANCE AND BODY STRUCTURE: Average, compact body, brownish or fresh complexion, dark hair. Rules abdominal and umbilical region, duodenum and intestines.

TEMPERAMENT: Intensely active mentally, a Virgo person has the faculty for acquiring knowledge. He loves to deal with facts rather than theories. He inclines to statistics and is often a walking encyclopedia of information. Being studious, scientific and mentally alert, he is never satisfied until he knows how desired results may be obtained. His thoughts, feelings and actions are always motivated by analysis.

Because he is practical and worldly, he can easily assume objectivity. Therefore, he makes an exceptional confidant. But do not expect him to solve your problem instantly. His careful, serious and contemplative approach to everything he does requires time. If given the necessary time to assimilate all the factors, his ingenuity allows him to impart helpful suggestions. He has the inherent ability of placing things in their proper order.

Dependable, industrious and conscientious, he can be trusted. He takes orders readily and uses skill and originality in carrying them out. This, in addition to his best quality of analysis, makes him exceptionally valuable to executives who do planning. For that matter, he can discern the many facets of a proposition and detect its weaknesses and determine how they can be strengthened.

A Virgo person is severely discriminative. And because he is constantly analyzing for the purpose of discrimination, he is inclined to be critical, his worst quality. He is apt to judge with severity the flaws in other people as well as their plans. He should utilize his keen judgment to look for the good points in people and in things rather than looking for objectionable qualities. This constructive approach will prove more profitable to him.

PERSONAL INTERESTS: Affairs concerned with sickness, labor, servants, co-workers, inferiors, tenants, farmers, small animals, poultry, foods, army, navy, police, and ceremonial or other magic performed by the querent.

OCCUPATIONS: Accountants, analytical chemists, animal trainers, appraisers, broadcasting technicians, data processors, dental hygienists, dental technicians, dietitians, draftsmen, druggists, dry cleaners, efficiency experts, food checkers, hygienists, industrial hygienists, inspectors, mathematicians, medical stenographers, microbiologists, nurses, osteopaths, pattern makers, pharmacists, physical chemists, piano tuners, plasma physicists, servants, statisticians, technical illustrators, textile workers, veterinarians, waiters.

SIGNIFICANT ASSOCIATIONS: Number 2. Letter B. Color dark violet. Tone low B. Gem jasper. Mineral flint stone. Herbs such as barley, oats, rye, wheat, privet, succory, skullcap, woodbine, valerian, millet and endive.

ENVIRONMENTAL FACTORS: Climate: Cold, moderate rainfall. Country: moderately elevated. Land: devoted to grass, fields, orchards, or other crops. City: public works, grocery stores, produce markets, agencies, restaurants and cafeterias. Home: pantry, garden, dining room, sick room, sewing basket, sewing machine, menus, recipe files, the bar, refrigerator, places where food is kept, and places where pets are kept.

CITIES OF THE WORLD: AUSTRALIA, Brisbane, Newcastle, Rockhampton, Sydney, Toowoomba. ISLANDS, Gilbert, Marshall, New Caledonia, Solomon, Wake. NEW ZEALAND, Auckland, Christchurch, Dunedin, Gisborne, Wellington. SOVIET UNION, Ambarchik, Anadyr, Magadan, Pepropavlovsk, Seymchan.

UNITED STATES OF AMERICA: California.

WORLD AFFAIRS: Associated with matters dependent upon the illness of the people of a country or city, their food; laboring people, their labor and working conditions, employees in general, including the personnel of the army, navy and police force, who are employees of the people. Also all civil service employees, stored grain or other stored products of the land or mines, the garnered harvest, restaurants, cafeterias, drug stores, and all places where food and drink are dispensed.

LIBRA

APPEARANCE AND BODY STRUCTURE: Tall and well formed, clear complexion, sparkling eyes, hair brown or black. Rules the lumbar region, kidneys, seed, reproductive fluids, and the internal generative organs.

TEMPERAMENT: A Libra person has a deep love of justice, peace and harmony, and is noted for his even temper. He so dislikes to hurt another's feelings that he can seldom say no. He should learn that he will be better liked by others in the long run if he has the character to render firm decisions.

He is not a loner but craves companionship in all of his activities. He is courteous and kind and deeply craves understanding. He finds social relations essential to his happiness and therefore should not live an isolated life. For this reason, he has a strong desire to make friends. Due to his insistent social desires and his sensitive nature, he should choose his companions carefully. His selection should be based on whether others lift or lower his mood.

The first impression he gives is one of charm and grace. Having refinement and dignity, when he is expressing his best quality of affability, he is quickly welcomed into any group. He seems poised at all times. But due to his difficulty in making decisions, he is not as confident as he may appear. This accounts for his worst quality, a love of flattery. He is so easily influenced by others that this can lead him into a trap. He can quickly regain his equilibrium by developing his own judgment rather than depending upon false praise.

Being somewhat changeable, he has a tendency to dabble in many things and thus scatter his energies. In this age of specialization, he would be wise to narrow his activities and not spread himself too thin. In this manner he will be able to focus his creative talents to greater accomplishment.

PERSONAL INTERESTS: Activities dealing with companionship, partners, the mate, the public, lawsuits, open enemies, contracts, sweethearts, doctors.

OCCUPATIONS: Beauticians, confectioners, cosmeticians, dressmakers, florists, furriers, haberdashers, interior decorators, milliners, musicians, painters and decorators, receptionists, tailors, wig makers.

SIGNIFICANT ASSOCIATIONS: Number 3. Letter G. Color light shades of yellow. Tone high E. Gem diamond. Stones white quartz, white spar, white marble. Herbs such as white rose, strawberry, violet, watercress, primrose, balm, pansy, and lemon-thyme.

ENVIRONMENTAL FACTORS: Climate: temperate. Country: high and dry. Land: rather thickly settled and divided into numerous plots, or where there are towns and villages. City: stores where wearing apparel, jewelry and finery are sold, show windows, and all places where attractive things are on display. Home: clothes closets, bedrooms, balconies, porches, chinaware and silverware, jewel cases, dressing tables, cosmetics, flowers, and places where sweets are kept.

CITIES OF THE WORLD: ALASKA, Nome, St Michael. ALEUTIANS, Dutch Harbor. ISLANDS, Hawaiian, Midway

UNITED STATES OF AMERICA: None.

WORLD AFFAIRS: Associated with matters dependent upon foreign nations and their attitudes, war and international affairs, marriage, divorce.

SCORPIO

APPEARANCE AND BODY STRUCTURE: Middle height, thick set, corpulent, hooked nose, dark hair, ruddy or swarthy complexion. Rules the nose, pelvis of the kidneys, ureters, bladder, sigmoid flexure, rectum, prostate gland, uterus and the external generative organs.

TEMPERAMENT: A Scorpio person has a never failing fund of ideas and resources and an abundant life-giving magnetism.

This magnetism makes him an excellent natural healer and often enables him to become a successful surgeon. Having intense likes and dislikes, whatever he finds to do he does with all his might.

At times he appears to be cold, calculating, and unsympathetic, but this manner could be easily misunderstood. He takes an active interest in people as individuals, studying their actions to learn what makes one person different from another. His interest in others may stem from the fact that he has a complex personality and varied talents himself.

All of his emotions are deep and strong, boiling the moment an avenue of escape is found. Regardless of how he expresses his tremendous force, he exerts great pressure upon his environment. And as people form a part of his realistic atmosphere, they could easily become targets when he is crossed. Then he becomes shrewd, suspicious, jealous and is out to get even.

Because his best quality is resourcefulness, it comes natural for him to assume positions of trust and responibility. Due to his ability to organize ideas and plans, he is never phased by difficult problems. He can be trusted to grapple with the most complicated and disagreeable tasks. His probing mind enables him to work out possibilities for more efficiency.

On his worst side, he becomes troublesome by insisting that others conduct themselves in what he considers the proper manner. He should learn that sometimes his success depends upon his willingness to take second place, and that asking questions is not an indication of inferiority. He should move with the world's mental current rather than oppose it.

PERSONAL INTERESTS: Affairs concerned with the partner's money, the public's money, legacies, real or personal property while in escrow, insurance, mortgages, plumbing, conditions surrounding death, psychic influences.

OCCUPATIONS: Aerodynamicists, bail bondsmen, bill collectors, butchers, claims adjusters, computer programmers, dentists, detectives, embalmers, funeral directors, gynecologists, infrared specialists, inorganic chemists, insurance agents, liquor dealers, locksmiths, market research analysts, medical laboratory technicians, medical x-ray technicians, paleontologists, physicians, plumbers, psychiatrists, radiobiologists, tax consultants.

SIGNIFICANT ASSOCIATIONS: Number 4. Letter D. Color darker shades of red. Tone low C. Gem Spanish topaz. Stones bloodstone, vermilion, lodestone. Herbs such as heather, horehound, bramble, bean, leek, wormwood, woad, charlock, blackthorn.

ENVIRONMENTAL FACTORS: Climate: damp and sultry. Country: rather low than high, away from the ocean and in a valley between hills. Land: where there are bogs, hot springs, quagmires, swamps, stagnant water and muddy ground. City: drug stores, doctors' offices, morgues, slaughter houses, sewers and cesspools. Home: medicine chest and first-aid kit, bathroom, the sewer and plumbing.

CITIES OF THE WORLD: ALASKA, Anchorage, Fairbanks, Juneau, Ketchikan. CALIFORNIA, Chico, Modesto, Monterey, Oakland, Redding, Sacramento, Salinas, San Francisco, San Jose, Santa Cruz, Santa Rosa, Stockton, Eureka. CANADA, Aklavik, Dawson, Dawson Creek, Mackenzie, Prince Rupert, Simpson, Vancouver, Victoria. ISLAND, Tahiti. OREGON, Coos Bay, Grants Pass, Klamath Falls, Medford, Portland, Salem. WASHINGTON, Bellingham, Everett, Olympia, Seattle, Tacoma, Yakima.

UNITED STATES OF AMERICA: Montana, Nevada, North Carolina, North Dakota, Oklahoma, South Dakota, Washington.

WORLD AFFAIRS: Associated with matters dependent upon the death rate and the kind of deaths suffered by the people, debts due from foreign countries, tariffs, taxes, insurance, pensions, the cabinet of the president or prime minister, chief appointees of the city mayor or state governor.

SAGITTARIUS

APPEARANCE AND BODY STRUCTURE: Above middle height, high forehead, long nose, sanguine complexion, brown hair. Rules hips, thighs and sciatic nerve.

TEMPERAMENT: The motivation of a Sagittarian springs neither from complete intellect nor complete emotion. His expression results from a blending of both. He is never deceived by appearances and instinctively employs sound judgment. In spite of his idealistic nature, he is not just a dreamer but one who has the ability to pull his ideals down to a practical level.

Even though he can both give and take orders, he is a natural executive. His talents express best in a friendly atmosphere. In both thought and action, he goes straight to the point, caring more for effectiveness than elegance. Being aggressive and impulsive, his frank and outspoken nature should be curbed so that he will not offend others.

Due to his strong intuition, he can quickly size up and act upon opportunities as fast as they present themselves. But when he is tired or tense, he is apt to make snap judgments and jump to conclusions. If he does not relieve his high-strung nature with open-air recreation, he becomes a victim of bursts of temper and fits of nerves.

Since he is philosophically inclined and enthusiastic in his approach, he quickly throws off moods of morbid self-examination. His inherent adaptability, joviality and love of freedom allows him plenty of opportunity to rise above any depressing thoughts. His sincerity and kindheartedness lead him to be charitable to others, and he is quick to fight for their rights. His best quality is loyalty.

His worst characteristic is sportiveness. When restlessness takes hold, he abandons his native good judgment and becomes wanton. Then he is likely to act in a ludicrous, whimsical and facetious manner. His sportiveness often prompts him to engage in undesirable games of chance. Instead, he should find a work in life that is so interesting to him that it becomes a game in which success is the hazard.

PERSONAL INTERESTS: Affairs concerned with the public expression of opinions, advertising, publishing, dreams, long trips, philosophy, religion, books, schooling, visions, legal matters.

OCCUPATIONS: Advertising men, airline hostesses, airplane pilots, book publishers, broadcasting engineers, clergymen, flight engineers, interpreters, lawyers, lecturers, lifeguards, missile engineers, newspaper editors, philosophers, physical education instructors, playground directors, publicity directors, public relations men, radar technicians, radio announcers, ship radio operators, teachers, telegraph operators, television technicians, travel agents, traveling salesmen.

SIGNIFICANT ASSOCIATIONS: Number 7. Letter Z. Color light purple. Tone high A. Talismanic gem red garnet. Stones mixed with red and green such as turquoise. Herbs such as mallow, wood betony, featherfew and agrimony.

ENVIRONMENTAL FACTORS: Climate: hot, dry. Country: mountainous, moderately high. Land: covered with woods. City: churches, lecture halls, courthouses, lawyers' offices, book stores, book publishing establishments, and places for meeting of community welfare workers. Home: upstairs rooms, the chimney, stables, garage, altars or places of religious activity, and sports equipment.

CITIES OF THE WORLD: ARIZONA, Phoenix, Tucson. CALIFORNIA, Beverly Hills, Long Beach, Los Angeles, San Diego, Santa Barbara. CANADA, Churchill, Port Nelson, Regina, Winnipeg. COLORADO, Denver. GUATEMALA, Guatemala City. LOUISIANA, New Orleans. MEXICO, Acapulco, Baja California, Chihuahua, Guadalajara, La Paz, Mexico City, Monterrey, Puebla, Tampico, Vera Cruz. MINNESOTA, Minneapolis, St. Paul. MISSOURI,

Kansas City, St. Louis. NEBRASKA, Omaha. NEVADA, Las Vegas, Reno. OKLAHOMA, Oklahoma City, Tulsa. TENNESSEE, Memphis. TEXAS, Dallas, El Paso, Fort Worth, Houston, San Antonio. UTAH, Salt Lake City.

UNITED STATES OF AMERICA: Alabama, Delaware, Illinois, Indiana, Mississippi, New Jersey, Ohio, Pennsylvania.

WORLD AFFAIRS: Associated with national matters dependent upon interstate and international commerce and traffic, the navy, foreign shipping, interstate airplane traffic, the law, lawyers, the supreme court, churches, religion, preachers, teachers, publishing, advertising, books, lectures, and all places where opinions are publicly proclaimed.

CAPRICORN

APPEARANCE AND BODY STRUCTURE: Slender rather than stout, thin face, black hair, dark complexion. Rules the region of the knees.

TEMPERAMENT: The Capricorn person is highly ambitious for worldly success, wealth and station. Being a good organizer, he has the faculty for bringing together dissenting factions for synthesis and economy. He is at his best when given responsibility, and he can shoulder it successfully. Patient and persistent, he employs concentrated effort and skillful maneuvering to climb all but insurmountable obstacles.

Although humbly submissive to those in power, he persistently strives to gain power himself so that others may bend the knee to him. Capricorn adapts to every requirement to gain its end. He is ever alert to take advantage of the weaknesses of other people, using them either for his own selfish gain or for what he thinks is best for society as a whole. Being extremely practical and frugal, he dislikes waste of any kind, whether material or mental.

If you want to capture his attention, plan how you will

approach him. Even though he is a good reasoner, he assimilates slowly. So present your facts one at a time in a detailed manner. Do not expect him to enthuse over your ideas for his deliberate and cautious mind needs time to mull over the facts.

A Capricorn person can tell you the quality brand names of almost any merchandise, direct you to the best places in town to eat, or describe the latest in elegant attire. Conservative by nature, he is strongly conditioned by tradition. These influences form the threads of his personality. He knows how and when to say the correct thing in order to create the right impression. When he is expressing his higher side, he is a true diplomat.

When he is not functioning at his best, he sometimes becomes deceitful. In his tendency to use other people as stepping-stones to get to the goal he regards as important, he can easily adopt this trait. He should realize that the greatest advantage any person can have is integrity of character and devotion to the welfare of others.

PERSONAL INTERESTS: Affairs concerned with credit, honor, reputation, rank, trade or profession, business qualifications or affairs, the boss, superiors or those of unusual power.

OCCUPATIONS: Architects, bricklayers and masons, buyers, carpenters, ceramic engineers, chiropractors, civil engineers, civil service workers, cryogenic engineers, economists, FBI agents, housekeepers, industrial engineers, janitors, laborers, landlords, leather workers, mining engineers, nuclear safety engineers, personnel workers, plasterers, public health nutritionists, purchasing agents, radiation testers, traffic managers, vocational counselors, watchmen.

SIGNIFICANT ASSOCIATIONS: Number 8. Letter H, Ch. Color dark blue. Tone low G. Talismanic gem onyx, sardonyx and ash-colored or black minerals such as coal. Herbs such as henbane, nightshade and black poppy.

ENVIRONMENTAL FACTORS: Country: well up in rugged mountains, where there are rocks and brush but few large trees. Climate: cold with considerable snowfall. Land: suitable for mining, where the soil is poor and weeds and thorns are in abundance. City: city hall, chamber of commerce and the business district in general. Home: the office, the attic, the cellar and all dark places, air conditioning and places where ice or cold is used.

CITIES OF THE WORLD: ALABAMA, Birmingham. BOLIVIA, La Paz, Sucre, Trinidad. BRITISH HONDURAS, Belize. CANADA, Goose Bay, Montreal, Ottawa, Quebec, Toronto. CHILE, Puntaarenas, Santiago. COLUMBIA, Bogota. CONNECTICUT, Bridgeport, Hartford. COSTA RICA, San Jose. CUBA, Havana. DISTRICT OF COLUMBIA, Washington. ECUADOR, Quito. EL SALVADOR, San Salvadore. FLORIDA, Fort Myers, Jacksonville, Miami, Orlando, Palm Beach, Pensacola, Tampa, West Palm Beach. GEORGIA, Atlanta. HONDURAS, Tegucigalpa. ILLINOIS, Chicago. INDIANA, Indianapolis. ISLAND, Bermuda Isles. KENTUCKY, Louisville. MARYLAND, Baltimore. MASSACHUSETTS, Boston, Holyoke, Springfield, Worcester. MICHIGAN, Detroit, Flint, Grand Rapids. NEW JERSEY, Jersey City, Newark. NEW YORK, Albany, Brooklyn, Buffalo, New York, Rochester, Syracuse, Troy. NICARAGUA, Managua. OHIO, Akron, Cincinnati, Cleveland, Columbus, Dayton, Toledo, Warren, Youngstown. PENNSYLVANIA, Philadelphia, Pittsburgh. PERU, Lima. REPUBLIC OF PANAMA, Panama City. RHODE ISLAND, Providence. TENNESSEE, Nashville. VENEZUELA, Caracas. VIRGINIA, Norfolk, Portsmouth, Richmond. WISCONSIN, Milwaukee.

UNITED STATES OF AMERICA: Alaska, Connecticut, Georgia, Iowa, New Mexico, Texas, Utah.

WORLD AFFAIRS: Associated with national matters dependent upon the administration, president, dictator, monarch, governor or mayor, the credit and reputation of a nation, its business and its influence in world affairs, also eminent and famous persons, and those possessing unusual power.

AQUARIUS

APPEARANCE AND BODY STRUCTURE: Stout, well set, fair skin, sanguine complexion, pleasant. Rules the legs below the knees, and ankles.

TEMPERAMENT: An Aquarian person is progressive and usually possesses more advanced ideas than his companions. Although he is one of the most impersonal signs, he is usually pleasant, friendly, and cheerful. He knows just what to say and do to produce a given effect upon those with whom he is associated. He can be an interesting conversationalist because of his interest in education, new discoveries, the latest developments of science and invention—as well as current events. He finds it easier to learn from hearing others talk than through the study of books.

He functions more on the mental plane rather than on the emotional. Thus, his unconventional and broad outlook sponsor practical activities along creative lines. He is well known for his interest in the very old or the very new. He has the ability to blend art and science into meaningful concepts, or to devise ultra-modern uses for items which hit the junk heap years ago.

He seeks the society of others because he loves the interchange of ideas. Having strong likes and dislikes, he frequently will take the opposite side of a question merely for the sake of discussion. Sometimes this leads him to his worst quality—argumentation. If he carries this attitude too far, he may be rejected. Then he develops a nervous irritability and expounds such wild ideas that he invites his own downfall.

When he is in a positive mood, his purposes and aims are altruistic. This feeling of well-being gives him the urge to solve all the problems of the world. He is greatly concerned with politics and religion and tends to view them from the standpoint of the welfare of society as a whole. However, his enthusiasm is apt to be too greatly expended in theoretically solving the difficulties of mankind rather than in efficient action. He should learn that wisdom must be accompanied by practical application if he is to accomplish anything worth while.

PERSONAL INTERESTS: Affairs concerned with hopes, wishes, friends, counselors, acquaintances, praise, and friendly criticism.

OCCUPATIONS: Airconditioning technicians, astrobiologists, astrologers, astronomers, drapery hangers, electrical engineers, electricians, electronic technicians, electroplaters, furniture salesmen, inventors, nuclear physicists, psychologists, plastic workers, scientists, social workers, space physicists, visco-elasticians.

SIGNIFICANT ASSOCIATIONS: Number 9. Letter Th. Color sky blue. Tone high G. Talismanic gem blue sapphire. Such stones as obsidian and black pearl. Herbs such as myrrh, frankincense and spikenard.

ENVIRONMENTAL FACTORS: Country: neither low nor high, thickly settled, including cities. Climate: temperate, but changeable weather. Land: not rugged, yet with an artistic view, and chiefly used for human habitation. City: art stores, furniture stores, electrical lighting systems and places where automobiles, airplanes and radios are sold and their accessories obtained. Home: electric meter, electric lights, electrical appliances, radio, reception room, stairs, large furniture, stereo, television, artistic things on the wall, and the car.

CITIES OF THE WORLD: ARGENTINA, Buenos Aires. BRAZIL, Belem, Recife, Rio de Janeiro, Salvadore, Sao Luis, Sao Paulo. BRITISH GUIANA, Georgetown, Paramaribo. FRENCH GUIANA, Cayenne. GREENLAND, Godhavn, Godthaab, Julianehaab. NEW-

FOUNDLAND, Gander, St. John's. PARAGUAY, Asuncion. URA-
GUAY, Montevideo.

UNITED STATES OF AMERICA: Arizona, Kansas, Massachusetts,
Michigan, Oregon.

WORLD AFFAIRS: Associated with matters dependent upon the
legislature or parliament, particularly the Congress, the House
of Commons, the aldermen of a city, and ambassadors sent to
foreign countries.

PISCES

APPEARANCE AND BODY STRUCTURE: Tending to shortness,
fleshy, pale face, brown or dark hair, fishy eyes. Rules the feet
and toes.

TEMPERAMENT: Impressionable to his surroundings, a Pisces
person should constantly guard his thoughts, feelings and
actions. Sensitive and psychic, he tunes in on everything in his
environment, good or bad. Because he is inclined to be plastic,
unless he makes an effort to keep tuned to the good, he can
easily be dragged down by the weight of his negative thinking.

He can easily slip into moods of self-pity and think that all
the world is against him. If he indulges these thoughts too
long, he can quickly exhaust his nervous energy. For this reason, he should be thoroughly interested in and enthusiastic
about what he is doing, especially his choice of work.

No other sign has such extremes of temperament as Pisces.
Aside from his susceptibility toward despondency and his inability to take it on the chin, he is just as easily stimulated to
express the other extreme of the emotional gamut. Then he has
a tendency to babble with enthusiasm and vibrate with
excitement.

He is generously endowed with many fine inner traits—
refined ideas, lofty characteristics and idealistic thoughts. He
responds best to peace and harmony and cringes in the face of

an impersonal, aggressive, slam-bang atmosphere. His warmth and compassion lead to his best quality—sympathy.

He has a tendency to build frustrations when he expresses his worst quality—worry. Being sensitive to discords and to the thoughts of others, he is inclined to magnify the importance of slight adversity, or imagine problems that never come to pass. He should curb his vivid imagination and face reality.

Instead of wasting his energies in worrying about what other people think of him, he should use them in a creative channel to express his varied talents. To work effectively, he must cultivate the faculty of finishing everything he starts.

PERSONAL INTERESTS: Affairs concerned with private enemies, disappointments, sorrows, psychic influences, magic (either white or black) performed by another, detective work, prisons, hospitals, charitable institutions and self injury. Restrictions, limitations, unseen forces, relation of astral entities.

OCCUPATIONS: Bartenders, chemical engineers, dancers, divers, fishermen, hospital attendants, occultists, oceanographers, oil-field workers, organic chemists, photographers, seamen, shoemakers, shoe salesmen.

SIGNIFICANT ASSOCIATIONS: Number 12. Letter L. Color dark purple. Tone low A. Talismanic gem peridot. Such stones as sand, gravel, pumice and coral. Herbs such as mosses which grow in the water, ferns and seaweed.

ENVIRONMENTAL FACTORS: Country: moderately low and much broken, shut in on all sides by hills and cut up by ravines. Climate: cool, rainy, foggy. Land: around fishponds or through which large rivers or small, sluggish creeks flow, or near large lakes, or where there are cool springs of water coming from the ground. City: hospitals, jails, poorhouses and public charities. Home: sinks, gas systems, gas appliances, gas meter, poisons, fishing tackle, and places where shoes are kept.

CITIES OF THE WORLD: EIRE, Cork, Dublin. ENGLAND, Birmingham, Brighton, Bristol, Liverpool, London, Manchester, Northampton, Nottingham, Oxford, Plymouth, Portsmouth, Sheffield. FRANCE, Bordeau, Nantes. GAMBIA, Bathurst. GHANA, Accra. GUINEA, Conakry. ICELAND, Reykjavik. IRELAND, Belfast, Londonderry. IVORY COAST, Abidjan. LIBERIA, Monrovia. MALI, Bamako. MAURITANIA, Nouakchott. MOROCCO, Casablanca. PORTUGAL, Lisbon. SCOTLAND, Dundee, Edinburgh, Glasgow, Newcastle-on-Tyne. SENEGAL, Dakar. SIERRA LEONE, Freetown. SPAIN, Cartagena, Grenada, La Coruna, Madrid, Santander, Sebastian, Seville, Valencia. UPPER VOLTA, Ouagadougou. WALES, Cardiff.

UNITED STATES OF AMERICA: Florida, Maine, Nebraska, Vermont.

WORLD AFFAIRS: Associated with national matters dependent upon prisons, hospitals, asylums, workhouses, charitable institutions, relief work, crime, criminals, detectives, secret societies, spies and the secret enemies of the people.

SUN

APPEARANCE AND BODY STRUCTURE: A strong vital body, above average size, light complexion, dignified manner. Rules the vitality, spleen, heart, spine, the front pituitary gland, and part of the thyroid gland.

TEMPERAMENT: The Sun represents the power thought urges which express as the drive for significance. A Sun-type person has a great deal of self esteem. He is paternal, considerate, firm and unbending, proud, conscientious, kindly, gracious, moderately liberal, and likes to control others. He is also fond of praise. He really doesn't like to work for others unless he is given full charge of his department. When he is expressing his highest potential, his best quality, rulership, comes out when he is at the head of something. On the other hand, as his worst quality is dictativeness, he should learn that taking over or assuming superiority by himself weakens his authority. If he is more considerate of the opinions of others and expresses sympathy with their views, he will get more cooperation.

PERSONAL INTERESTS: Those concerned with people in authority, politicians, the government, the vital forces, the male sex, children and speculation. Actions involving the good will of those in authority, and in seeking a position or promotion. All affairs concerning health and vitality.

OCCUPATIONS: Biochemists, entertainers, financiers, foremen, playground directors, politicians, radiation testers, supervisors, theatre managers, ushers.

SIGNIFICANT ASSOCIATIONS: Number 21. Letter B. Color orange. Tone D. Metal gold. Flower helianthus and gallardia. Reacts best to light and color.

ENVIRONMENTAL FACTORS: Gold, politics, persons of authority, the male sex in general and those who employ others.

WORLD AFFAIRS: In thought, politics. In business, executive work and administration. In politics, bosses and the ruling class or those in power.

PERSONAL ABILITY: Inclines to official positions, civil or political, or to deputies appointed by office holders. Predisposes to become head of something, even if only over a few people, such as a shop foreman or the head of a small department in some business.

MOON

APPEARANCE AND BODY STRUCTURE: Tending to shortness and weight, pale complexion, wide forehead, listless. Rules the constitutional magnetism, influences medulla oblongata and base of brain, fluidic and lymphatic system, and has influence over the eyes. Action of back pituitary gland, thymus gland, and the hormones of the alimentary tract.

TEMPERAMENT: The Moon represents the domestic thought urges whose nature is best expressed in one word as impressionable. A Moon-type person has a love of notoriety. He enjoys being before the public or rubbing shoulders with many people. His best quality is adaptability. However, due to his changeable, negative, and dreamy nature, he should guard against the development of his worst quality, inconstancy. He should recognize the fact that if he desires to become famous and be adored by the public, he will have to stick to one endeavor in order to develop exceptional ability. Because he is inoffensive and lacking in force, he appears to be shy and timid, but in dealing with him, one should remember his sensitive nature and approach him accordingly.

PERSONAL INTERESTS: Affairs concerned with the common people, nurses, liquids, groceries, the home, music in general and women.

OCCUPATIONS: Airplane hostesses, bakers, caretakers, cashiers, cooks, dietitians, dry cleaners, grocers, hospital attendants, housekeepers, landscapers, laundry workers, merchants, meteorologists, milkmen, nurses, obstetricians, restaurant managers.

SIGNIFICANT ASSOCIATIONS: Number 20. Letter R. Color green. Tone F. Metal silver. Flower lily. Reacts best to hydro-therapy.

ENVIRONMENTAL FACTORS: Silver, liquids, commodities, hotels, the home, food, the common people, the female sex in general, and music.

WORLD AFFAIRS: In thought, the family and home. In business, groceries and other commodities. In politics, women and the common people. Tends to affect the masses.

PERSONAL ABILITY: Inclines to everyday business in the retail trade, to fishing, seamanship, nursing and to serving food. Best when meeting large numbers of all kinds of people.

MERCURY

APPEARANCE AND BODY STRUCTURE: Lean, nervous, sharp features, small eyes and ears, hair brown. Rules the brain and nervous system, nerve currents, mouth, tongue, parathyroid gland activity, and part of front pituitary.

TEMPERAMENT: Mercury represents the intellectual thought urges so closely tied in with perception and expression. A Mercury-type person is quick, witty, ingenious, intelligent, scientific, changeable, persuasive and enterprising. His curious nature gives him an interest in language, calculation, and the recognition of size, weight, form and color. He has a bright, changeable personality and loves to talk. He is at his best when he can get what he wants by writing, talking or traveling. His worst quality is restlessness. Therefore, he should recognize that results are not always forthcoming when a speedy approach is used. He can express his best mentality with proper concentration.

PERSONAL INTERESTS: Activities dependent upon writers, students, writing, printing, speaking, teaching, contracts, travel and mental work in general. Those concerned with fluency of speech, clear thinking, or an alert mind.

OCCUPATIONS: Analytical chemists, animal trainers, bank tellers, bookbinders, book editors, broadcasting technicians, bus drivers, cab drivers, canvassers, clerk-typists, computer programmers, desk clerks, drapery hangers, elevator operators, food checkers, graphologists, hygienists, IBM operators, inspectors, interpreters, lecturers, librarians, mail carriers, manicurists, medical stenographers, messengers, navigators, news boys, newspaper reporters, optometrists, osteopaths, porters, printers, radio announcers, railroad men, receptionists, secretaries, servants, service station attendants, shipping and receiving clerks, solicitors, stenographers, teachers, telephone operators, ticket agents, travel agents, typesetters, veterinarians, waiters, weather observers, writers.

SIGNIFICANT ASSOCIATIONS: Number 1. Letter A. Color violet. Tone B. Metal quick silver. Flower jasmine and honeysuckle. Mineral the metal mercury. Reacts best to mental treatments.

ENVIRONMENTAL FACTORS: Books, railroads, periodicals, telephone and telegraph systems, and people who are literary or studious.

WORLD AFFAIRS: In thought, science. In business, literary work. In politics, the press. When prominent, shows much talk, and usually some controversy.

PERSONAL ABILITY: Inclines to talking, writing, traveling, teaching and the constant use of the mind. Clerical work, accounting, postal work, traveling salesman or acting as an agent. An opportunity to express the mentality.

VENUS

APPEARANCE AND BODY STRUCTURE: Plump and handsome, tending to light complexion, mirthful, affable. Rules the venous blood, veins, skin, hair, and the action of the thyroid gland and the gonad glands.

TEMPERAMENT: Venus represents the social thought urges often expressing as attraction and affection. A Venus-type person is friendly, yielding and submissive, affectionate, easily given to laughter and companionable. His clinging and receptive nature makes him coy, shy and sensitive. In seeking harmony, he is too desirous of pleasing others and tends to follow the line of least resistance. This leads to his worst quality, pliancy. To be at his best, he demands companionship. Unfitted for a life of solitude, he needs an atmosphere in which to express his amiability and conviviality.

PERSONAL INTERESTS: Activities associated with artists, social matters, friendship, love, marriage, singing, dancing, art, finery.

OCCUPATIONS: Beauticians, ceramic engineers, commercial artists, confectioners, dressmakers, florists, furriers, haberdashers, interior decorators, jewelers, milliners, occupational therapists, package designers, painters and decorators, receptionists, singers, textile workers, wig makers.

SIGNIFICANT ASSOCIATIONS: Number 6. Letters U, V, W. Color yellow. Tone E. Metal copper. Flower rose. Responds best to rest and relaxation.

ENVIRONMENTAL FACTORS: Flowers, art of all kinds, wearing apparel, fancy goods, confections, pastry, toilet articles, jewelry, perfume.

WORLD AFFAIRS: In thought, the artistic and beautiful. In business, art. In politics, the so-called social element. Trend is to events affecting women.

PERSONAL ABILITY: Avoids hard work, and depends upon affability, grace of manners and good taste to get by. More interested in pleasure than the practical aspect.

MARS

APPEARANCE AND BODY STRUCTURE: Wiry, robust body, strong muscles, ruddy complexion, hair with reddish tinge. Rules the muscular system, red corpuscles, gonad glands, and secretion of adrenalin and cortin by the adrenal glands.

TEMPERAMENT: Mars represents the aggressive thought urges which express as the drive for reproduction. A Mars-type person is not timid and knows no fear. He is sharp of tongue, impulsive, headstrong, and assertive. Because he must have an outlet for his abundant energy, his thoughtlessness could lead him into destructive activities. To prevent the expression of his worst quality, harshness, he should realize that greater personal satisfaction will come to him when he uses his creative energy to build rather than to tear down. He likes his freedom, and he likes to fight. To best express his highest quality of initiative, he should fight for some cause that will help mankind.

PERSONAL INTERESTS: Activities associated with doctors, surgeons, mechanics, soldiers, warfare, machinery, the use of steel and iron, and building and manufacturing in general.

OCCUPATIONS: Athletes, automobile mechanics, barbers, bill collectors, business machine repairmen, butchers, diamond cutters, divers, electroplaters, firemen, flight engineers, gynecologists, iron workers, lifeguards, liquor dealers, locksmiths, manufacturers, masseurs, mechanical engineers, medical laboratory technicians, missile engineers, office machine operators, physical education instructors, physical therapists, physicians, physiotherapists, propulsion technicians, sales agents, sheetmetal workers, soldiers, stationary engineers, surgeons, tool and die makers, tool designers, welders.

SIGNIFICANT ASSOCIATIONS: Number 16. Letter O. Color red. Tone C. Metal iron. Flower hollyhock. Mineral iron. Reacts best to thermo-therapeutics.

ENVIRONMENTAL FACTORS: Steel, machinery of all kinds, implements of construction and destruction, intoxicating drink, and among people, cooks, soldiers.

WORLD AFFAIRS: In thought, mechanics. In business, manufacturing and the military profession. In politics, militarism. Tends to strife, violence and accidents.

PERSONAL ABILITY: Aggressive, either destructive or constructive. Takes to all mechanical work, to war, to surgery. Needs outlet for abundant energy.

JUPITER

APPEARANCE AND BODY STRUCTURE: Large and ample body, sanguine or fair complexion, jovial, with much self-esteem. Rules the arterial system, liver, fats and glycogen, and the manufacture and secretion of insulin by the pancreas gland.

TEMPERAMENT: Jupiter represents the religious thought urges which underlie generosity, warmth, and expansion. A Jupiter-type person expresses benevolence, good cheer, honesty and discrimination. He gains his ends through patronage and favor. His radiant, jovial personality chafes under restraint. Outgoing and broadminded, he gravitates easily to the professions, where he usually expresses his best quality, benevolence. Having a good opinion of himself, he should hold an objective evaluation or this opinion may carry him into his worst quality of conceit. True charity demands that he give others due consideration.

PERSONAL INTERESTS: Activities dependent upon clergymen and professional work, legal matters, judges, charities, banking and bankers, publishing, religion and philosophy, finances, people of wealth, good will, salesmanship, patronage, merchandise and general good luck.

OCCUPATIONS: Advertising men, bail bondsmen, book publishers, clergymen, funeral directors, furniture salesmen, lawyers, philosophers, publicity directors, public relations men, shoe salesmen, stock brokers, traveling salesmen.

SIGNIFICANT ASSOCIATIONS: Number 5. Letter E. Color purple. Tone A. Metal tin. Flower dahlia. Reacts best to proper diet.

ENVIRONMENTAL FACTORS: Judges, clergymen, bankers, professional men of all kinds, merchandise and persons of wealth.

WORLD AFFAIRS: In thought, religion and philosophy. In business, finance and commerce. In politics, capitalism. Trend is toward expansion, expenditures and higher prices.

PERSONAL ABILITY: Inclines toward professions and things which appeal to the wealthy. Good salesmen. Noted for good fellowship and a genial personality.

SATURN

APPEARANCE AND BODY STRUCTURE: Large bones, looks rawboned even when not tall, serious, grave. Rules the spleen, bones, ligaments, teeth, mineral salts of the body, one hormone of the front pituitary gland, and action of adrenal glands.

TEMPERAMENT: Saturn represents the safety thought urges which express as the desire for security. A Saturn-type person is practical and concrete, collecting and hoarding the treasures of earth and the treasures of the mind. But things do not come to him easily. He works hard for all he gets. And whatever good comes from his influence is the result of carefully laid plans, plodding effort, subtlety, craft, and cunning. In his approach, he prefers not to take the initiative, but prefers to remain behind the scenes using innuendo rather than force. Due to his natural tendency to be reserved, fearful and melancholy, his worst trait is selfishness. He can prevent these moods by expressing his best quality of system. He can replace his timid and retiring traits by practicing efficiency, economy and organization, a few of his better traits.

PERSONAL INTERESTS: Activities associated with miners, farmers, common laborers, hard work, business in general, especially buying, mining, real estate, elderly people, agriculture and secret and hidden things.

OCCUPATIONS: Aerodynamicists, accountants, appraisers, architects, baby sitters, bankers, bookkeepers, bricklayers and masons, buyers, cabinet makers, carpenters, carpet layers, cartoonists, chiropractors, civil engineers, civil service workers, claims adjusters, cryogenic engineers, custodians, data processers, dental hygienists, dental technicians, dentists, draftsmen, economists, efficiency experts, farmers, foresters, gardeners, geologists, guards, historians, industrial engineers, industrial hygienists, inorganic chemists, insurance agents, janitors, laborers, landlords, leather workers, mathematicians, medical record librarians, microbiologists, mining engineers, newspaper editors, paleontologists, pattern makers, personnel workers, physical chemists, piano tuners, plasterers, proofreaders, shoemakers, statisticians, surveyors, tailors, tax consultants, type setters, upholsterers, vocational counselors, watchmen.

SIGNIFICANT ASSOCIATIONS: Number 15. Letter X. Color blue. Tone G. Metal lead. Flower statice. Reacts best to naturopathy.

ENVIRONMENTAL FACTORS: Basic utilities, such as minerals, hay, grain, coal and building materials. Mines, real estate, the land.

WORLD AFFAIRS: In thought, orthodoxy. In business, land and basic utilities. In politics, conservatism, the farmer, and the miner. Tends to influence labor and tends toward contraction, economy, loss and lower prices.

PERSONAL ABILITY: Depends upon foresight, system, economy, management and persistent labor. Inclines to sedentary work and to laborious work. Not a good direct-contact salesman, but can buy to advantage—a shrewd trader.

URANUS

APPEARANCE AND BODY STRUCTURE: Tall, slender, angular, brilliant eyes, erratic, argumentative. Rules the action of parathyroid gland and one hormone of the front pituitary gland; and the nervous system and nerve control, as it is associated with the potential and vibratory rate of the electrical energies generated by the nerves.

TEMPERAMENT: Uranus represents the individualistic thought urges often expressing as originality and independence. The Uranus-type person is inventive, often acts on impulse, and has a dynamic personal magnetism. Sometimes he appears to take a radical viewpoint, because his ideas are far ahead of the times. This progressive attitude leads to great enthusiasm when ideas of reformation come up. If carried too far, he expresses his worst quality, eccentricity. He should learn that moderate views are more apt to impress others with sanity of essential reform. If he controls his abrupt and erratic tendencies with the expression of his best quality of originality, his penetrative mind and intuitive faculties, coupled with his scientific bent, he will be able to come up with modern and useful concepts.

PERSONAL INTERESTS: Activities dependent upon lawyers, astrologers, unusual methods in business, astrology, occultism, invention, electricity and ingenious mechanisms, automobiles, radical ideas, exposures, reforms, and agitation.

OCCUPATIONS: Air conditioning technicians, astrologers, astronomers, electrical engineers, electricians, electronic technicians, inventors, metallurgical engineers, nuclear physicists, psychologists, plastics workers, psychiatrists, scientists, technical writers, telephone repairmen, visco-elasticians.

SIGNIFICANT ASSOCIATIONS: Number 10. Letters I, J, Y. Color dazzling white. Tone astral chimes. Flower clover and oxalis. Reacts best to electricity and mesmerism.

ENVIRONMENTAL FACTORS: Inventions, automobiles, late mechanical devices, orators, lawyers, electricians, astrology, occultists.

WORLD AFFAIRS: In thought, the occult and ultra-progressive. In politics, the radical element. In business, invention and unusual methods. Trend is toward radical activities and exposés.

PERSONAL ABILITY: Original, inventive, tends to the uncommon. Has power to influence others through magnetism. Needs an outlet for unusual ingenuity.

NEPTUNE

APPEARANCE AND BODY STRUCTURE: Tendency to weight, oval features, large dreamy eyes, pleasant appearing. Rules part of the parathyroid glands, the hormone of the pineal gland and toxins.

TEMPERAMENT: Neptune represents the utopian thought urges behind fantasy, idealism, and mediumistic qualities. The Neptune-type person is impressionable, being of a magnetic, psychic nature. He is dreamy and often believes in hopes that are seldom realized because his idealistic visions do not fit the mold of physical reality. A promoter of worldly schemes to gain wealth without work, his is subtle, theoretical and fanciful. Because he abhors critical analysis, he often becomes vague, his worst quality. So what he needs to build into his character is system and discipline. The only way in which his wonderful ideas can benefit himself and others is if his ideas can be put into practical use. In the social area, he could find himself involved in romantic attachments and platonic friendships. His attractive manner is mild and pleasant.

PERSONAL INTERESTS: Activities dependent upon actors, psychics, feeling ESP, promotions, involuntary servitude, stock companies, utopian ideas, dramatic expression in all mediums, aviation, submarines, gas, oil, drugs, and poisons.

OCCUPATIONS: Actors, airplane pilots, artists, bartenders, chemical engineers, cosmeticians, dancers, druggists, fashion designers, fishermen, industrial designers, makeup artists, market research analysts, musicians, oceanographers, occultists, oil-field workers, photoengravers, photographers, seamen, thermo-dynamicists.

SIGNIFICANT ASSOCIATIONS: Number 11. Letters C, K. Color changing iridescence. Tone music of the spheres. Metal neptunium. Flower arctotis. Reacts best to spiritual healing.

ENVIRONMENTAL FACTORS: Oil, gas, drugs, the drama, moving pictures, aviation, mediums, mystics, psychic people, and schemes requiring incorporation or the profit-sharing of a number of people.

WORLD AFFAIRS: In thought, the mystical and psychic. In business, promotion and stock companies. In politics, the ideal. Tends to events affecting aviation and the moving picture industry.

PERSONAL ABILITY: Visionary and dislikes physical work, but has the power to impart to others enthusiasm for his plans. Makes a good promoter, one who carries out psychic work of some nature, or who practices some progressive method of healing.

PLUTO

APPEARANCE AND BODY STRUCTURE: Average height, strong muscular body,deliberate but dynamic personality capable of expressing much force.

TEMPERAMENT: Pluto represents the universal welfare thought urges which are the motivating factors behind cooperation or coercion. Consciously or unconsciously, the Pluto-type person easily tunes in on the thoughts of others and impressions from the inner planes. This gives him an unusually wide source of information. When he expresses his lower nature, his resource-fulness and energy is turned against society. This explains his worst quality of inversion. It is then when he unites with others to spread subtle lies and prey upon humanity. In this mood he becomes drastic and violent. However, his best quality is spirituality, and when he is expressing it, he then relates to cooperative group effort of an aggressive nature that contributes to mankind as a whole.

PERSONAL INTERESTS: Concerned with people of great spiritual attainment, intellectual ESP, dictators, gangsters, spirituality, inversion, kidnapping, the inside of things, the inner plane and inner-plane activities, coercion, radio, television, groups, cooperation, group activities of all kinds.

OCCUPATIONS: Astrobiologists, broadcasting engineers, detectives, embalmers, FBI agents, infra-red specialists, medical x-ray technicians, nuclear safety engineers, plasma physicists, plumbers, policemen, public health nutritionists, radio operators, radar technicians, radiobiologists, ship radio operators, social workers, space physicists, telegraph operators, television technicians, traffic managers.

SIGNIFICANT ASSOCIATIONS: Number 22: Letter T. Color black, ultra-violet and infra-red. Tone spirit choir. Metal plutonium or soil of the earth. Flower pitcher plant. Reacts best to stellar healing.

ENVIRONMENTAL FACTORS: Television, the wireless transmission of messages or power, intra-atomic and cosmic sources of energy, the national planning, gangsters, kidnapping and compulsory codes for the benefit of the people as a whole.

WORLD AFFAIRS: In thought, spirituality or inversion and the influence of invisible intelligences. In business, group activity, either for selfish advantage of the group or for universal good. In politics, compulsory cooperation. Tends to bring events in which drastic action and cooperation of some kind play a part.

PERSONAL ABILITY: Requires close cooperation of a number of people, the regimentation of public opinion, cunning methods but can resort to force; uses latest discoveries and inventions to carry out a purpose.